A SURVEY OF THE RESEARCHES
INTO THE WESTERN TEXT
OF THE GOSPELS AND ACTS

SUPPLEMENTS
TO
NOVUM TESTAMENTUM

VOLUME XXI

LEIDEN
E. J. BRILL
1969

A SURVEY OF THE RESEARCHES
INTO THE WESTERN TEXT
OF THE GOSPELS AND ACTS

PART TWO
1949-1969

BY

A. F. J. KLIJN

LEIDEN
E. J. BRILL
1969

MAGISTRO · COLLEGAE · AMICO

per annos viginti

W. C. van UNNIK

hunc librum parvum
dedicavit
auctor

I should like to express my gratitude to the Reverend Canon G. Paul of Bristol, who having corrected Survey I twenty years ago, has again spent a great deal of time doing the same with Survey II.

CONTENTS

PREFACE

In 1959 I published two articles on the development of the inquiries into the Western Text of the Gospels and Acts during the years 1949 to 1959 [1]. They were meant to be a sequel to my book published in 1949 with the title *A Survey of the Researches into the Western Text of the Gospels and Acts* [2].

When I started to study the developments during the last ten years, I soon arrived at the conclusion that so many important discoveries had been made and so many valuable books and articles had appeared that a survey in the form of an article would be impossible. I had to choose the form of a book. In this book the inquiries during the years 1949 to 1969 have been incorporated so as to make it in the real sense of the word a second part of the first *Survey*.

The plan and the contents of this book have been dictated by the inquiries of the last twenty years. This means that some parts of the problem of the Western Text have received much more emphasis than other parts. This might seem to give an unbalanced character to this work. However, a glance at the contents shows that no region where the Western Text was used, has been omitted.

In addition to this we have tried to make this book more than a mere summary of other men's opinions. In many cases we have added our own contributions to the different problems. Finally, in the last chapter we hope to have offered an original contribution to the question of the origin of the Western Text. But we are obliged to say that this chapter could not have been written but for the findings of so many scholars who have devoted their energies to solving the age-old problem of the

Western Text of the Gospels and Acts.

---

[1] A. F. J. KLIJN, "A Survey of the Researches into the Western Text of the Gospels and Acts (1949-1959)", in: *NT* 3 1959, p. 1-27 and 161-173.
[2] A. F. J. KLIJN, *A Survey of the Researches into the Western Text of the Gospels and Acts*, Utrecht 1949.

LIST OF ABBREVIATIONS OF JOURNALS AND PERIODICALS

Bibl	Biblica
BJRL	Bulletin of the John Ryland's Library
BO	Biblica et Orientalia
BZ	Biblische Zeitschrift
CBQ	Catholic Biblical Quarterly
CSCO	Corpus Scriptorum Christianorum Orientalium
ET	Expository Times
GTT	Gereformeerd Theologisch Tijdschrift
HTR	Harvard Theological Review
JBL	Journal of Biblical Literature
JBR	Journal of Bible and Religion
JTS	Journal of Theological Studies
NRT	Nouvelle Revue Théologique
NT	Novum Testamentum
NTS	New Testament Studies
NTT	Nederlands Theologisch Tijdschrift
NTTS	New Testament Tools and Studies
OC	Oriens Christianus
RB	Revue Biblique
RSR	Recherches de Science Religieuse
S and D	Studies and Documents
T and S	Texts and Studies
TL	Theologische Literaturzeitung
TR	Theologische Rundschau
TS	Theological Studies
TU	Texte und Untersuchungen
VC	Vigiliae Christianae
VT	Vox Theologica
ZNW	Zeitschrift für die neutestamentliche Wissenschaft
ZTK	Zeitschrift für Theologie und Kirche

INTRODUCTION

The inquiries during the years 1949 to 1969 can be divided into two periods of about ten years each [1]. In the first ten years the result of work done in the previous decades was evaluated. This led to an intensive study of the Old Syriac text and a deeper penetration into the riddles of the Caesarean Text. Studies into the Diatessaron had reached their culminating point just a few years earlier and fell into the back-ground.

The second period was dominated by some spectacular discoveries. We only mention the papyri of the Bodmer Collection with large parts of the Gospels of John and Luke, the Syriac commentary of Ephrem on the Diatessaron in the Chester Beatty Collection, the Gospel of Thomas with its many "Words" of Jesus discovered among the important Gnostic writings from Nag Hammadi, and a Coptic Manuscript of Acts with a Western Text.

Textual critics were obliged to fit these discoveries into the picture they favoured of the history of the text. It appeared that this was not always possible. The history of the text in Egypt and Syria seemed to invite a fresh inquiry. This emphasis on the text in Syria and Egypt perhaps led to a lack of interest in the problems of the Latin text and the Caesarean text. In this book, however,

---

[1] During this period a number of survey-articles has appeared: E. Massaux, "État actuel de la Critique Textuelle du Nouveau Testament", in: *NRT* 69 1953, p. 703-726; B. M. Metzger, "A Survey of recent Research in the ancient Versions of the New Testament", in: *NTS* 2 1955/56, p. 1-16; J. Duplacy, "Où en est la Critique Textuelle du Nouveau Testament?", in: *RSR* 45 1957, p. 419-441; 46 1958, p. 270-316 and 431-462; K. Aland, "The present Position of New Testament Textual Criticism", in: *Studia Evangelica*, in: *TU* 73 1959, p. 717-731; K. Th. Schäfer, "Der Ertrag der textkritischen Arbeit am Neuen Testament seit der Jahrhundertwende", in: *BZ* n.F. 4 1960, p. 1-18, cf. K. Aland, "Eine Bemerkung zur gegenwärtigen Arbeit der neutestamentlichen Textkritik", in: *idem*, p. 315-318; H. H. Oliver, "Present Trends in the Textual Criticism of the New Testament", in: *JBR* 30 1962, p. 308-320; J. Duplacy, "Bulletin de Critique Textuelle du Nouveau Testament", in: *RSR* 50 1962, p. 242-263, 564-598; 51 1963, p. 432-462; J. Duplacy, "Bulletin de Critique Textuelle du Nouveau Testament II", in: *RSR* 53 1965, p. 257-284 and 54 1966, p. 426-476; H. K. Moulton, "The Present State of New Testament Textual Criticism", in: *The Bible Translator* 16 1965, p. 193-198; B. M. Metzger, "Bibliographic Aids for the Study of the Manuscripts of the New Testament", in: *Anglican Theol. Review* 48 1966, p. 339-355.

we hope to show that studies of the Syriac text and the Egyptian text have their bearing upon the Latin text and especially upon the Caesarean text.

In this introduction we may point to some important studies which do not deal with the Western Text in particular but nevertheless touch the problem in one way or another.

First of all we may mention three text-books on textual criticism written by V. Taylor [1], J. H. Greenlee [2], and B. M. Metzger [3]. The first two books are clearly meant for the average student. They give a good insight into the material and the practice of textual criticism. The book by Metzger gives valuable observations on the history of textual criticism. Otherwise, the contents of these books are not particular different from those in the text-books written sixty years ago.

We hope below to show something which was already becoming known, namely that the grouping of manuscripts into the four classical types of text which we still find referred to even in the modern text-books, is out of date. This grouping was the result of ideas which can no longer be accepted.

Next, we still get the impression from these books that one can speak about textual criticism without going into the origins of the Gospels. The more we go into the history of the text the more we notice the link between the problems of the text and those of the Gospel origins. In some articles it has been said that when Matthew and Luke incorporated Mark into their Gospels, the Gospel of Mark had already been modified by an occasional or even a thorough rewriting [4]. Inquiries into the quotations in the very early ecclesiastical authors show the importance of the period of oral tradition not only for the formation of the Gospels but also for the development of the text [5].

---

[1] V. TAYLOR, *The Text of the New Testament*, London 1961.

[2] J. H. GREENLEE, *Introduction to New Testament Textual Criticism*, Grand Rapids 1964.

[3] B. M. METZGER, *The Text of the New Testament, its Transmission, Correction and Restauration*, Oxford 1964 (sec. ed. 1968). We may add to this the earlier, but now partially revised works by F. C. KENYON, *The Text of the Greek Bible*, London 1947[2] and H. J. VOGELS, *Handbuch der Textkritik des Neuen Testaments*, Bonn 1955[2].

[4] Cf. J. PAIRMAN BROWN, "An early Revision of the Gospel of Mark", in: *JBL* 78 1959, p. 215-227, and J. F. GLASSON, "An early Revision of the Gospel of Mark", in: *idem* 85 1966, p. 231-233. See also O. LINTON, "Evidences of a second-century revised Edition of St. Mark's Gospel", in: *NTS* 14 1967/68, p. 321-355.

[5] E. FASCHER, *Textgeschichte als hermeneutisches Problem*, Halle 1953;

With these text-books we may mention a book written by Kieffer [1]. Starting from only a few verses in the Gospel of John, he tries to make a complete assessment of the available textual material and to show internal relationships. The results are forced into the classical types of text. This does not appear a satisfactory procedure. The author has also had to draw general conclusions from a very limited field of research.

A few editions of the Greek New Testament call for our attention. The Nestle-Aland-Editions has added to its apparatus the evidence of the newly discovered papyri, but the text still reflects the well known nineteenth century editions. A new edition of the text and apparatus is to be expected [2]. The edition of Merk has given the evidence of the papyri in an appendix. For those interested in the Western text it is good to know that in this edition the evidence of the Diatessaron has been cited in the apparatus [3]. The publication of the Greek text of the New English Bible is to be welcomed. It is an eclectic text which shows a great deal of agreement with the Nestle-Aland text. The appendix with notes on variant readings is very useful [4].

The Greek text published by the United Bible Societies serves a particular purpose. It is meant for translators who are presented with readings which are of any importance for our restoring of the original text. This means that only a limited number of variant readings are given in the apparatus. But in order to make a choice, the evidence of the different readings is given as fully as possible. In addition to this the variant readings are grouped according to their claim to be more or less in accordance with the original text [5].

M. Karnetzki, "Textgeschichte als Überlieferungsgeschichte", in: *ZNW* 47 1956, p. 160-180.

[1] R. Kieffer, "Au delà des Recensions? L'Évolution de la Tradition Textuelle dans Jean VI, 52-71", in: *Coniect. Biblica*, New Testament Series 3, Lund 1968.

[2] *Novum Testamentum Graece*, 25. Auflage 1963/1967. See also K. Aland, "The Greek New Testament: its present and future Editions", in: *JBL* 87 1968, p. 179-186.

[3] *Novum Testamentum Graece et Latinum*, ed. A. Merk, Roma 1964.

[4] *The Greek New Testament*, being the Text translated in the New English Bible 1961, ed. R. V. G. Tasker, Oxford-Cambridge 1964, cf. *Review* by A. F. J. Klijn, in: *NTS* 11 1964/65, p. 184-185, see also T. Gaumer, "An Examination of some Western textual Variants adopted in the Greek Text of the New English Bible", in: *The Bible Translator* 16 1965, p. 184-189.

[5] *The Greek New Testament*, ed. by Kurt Aland, Matthew Black, Bruce M. Metzger, Allen Wikgren, American Bible Society, British and Foreign Bible Society, National Bible Society of Scotland, Netherlands Bible Society,

Although this last edition is also based on the eclectic method [1], it also provides a text with only a few deviations from Nestle-Aland. This again proves that the אB text is still supposed to contain the greatest percentage of original readings. This, however, is not to say that the text as a whole is identical with the original text [2].

The joint English and American project to publish a Greek text with the greatest possible number of variant readings has published at last one page of Luke in order to show what the coming edition will look like. This proof sheet was, however, not very favourably received by Aland [3].

Finally we may mention a concordance of Greek words especially met with in readings particular to the Manuscript D. This work compiled by Yoder is very useful for every student of the Western Text [4].

Württemberg Bible Society 1966, cf. R. P. MARKHAM-E. A. NIDA, *An Introduction to the Bible Societies' Greek New Testament*, publ. by the Sponsoring Societies 1966, and *Review* by I. A. MOIR, in: *NTS* 14 1967 68, p. 136-143, see also K. ALAND, *The Greek New Testament* . . . We may also refer to the second edition of the Greek New Testament published by the British and Foreign Bible Society in 1958 with the text of 1904, but with a revised critical apparatus and *A Greek-English Diglot for the Use of Translators* published from 1959 in different parts by the same Society with an eclectic text.

[1] Cf. K. W. CLARK, "The Effect of recent Textual Criticism upon the New Testament Studies", in: D. W. DAVIES and D. DAUBE, *The Background of the New Testament . . . in hon. of C. H. Dodd*, Cambridge 1956, p. 21-51, p. 37: "The eclectic method is openly embraced in our day".

[2] See K. ALAND, "Neue Neutestamentliche Papyri II", in: *NTS* 12 1965/66, p. 193-210, who reopens the debate on the Western-non-Interpolations in the light of the ancient papyri recently discovered which have the interpolations, see also J. A. FITZMEYER, "Papyrus Bodmer II: Some Features of our oldest Text of Luke", in: *CBQ* 24 1962, p. 170-179, and E. C. COLWELL, "External Evidence and New Testament Textual Criticism", in: *Studies in the History and Text of the New Testament in honor of K. W. Clark* by B. L. DANIELS and M. J. SUGGS, in: *S and D* XXIX, Salt Lake City 1967, p. 1-12.

[3] See K. ALAND, "Bemerkungen zu Probeseiten einer groszen kritischen Ausgabe des Neuen Testaments", in: *Studien zur Überlieferung des Neuen Testaments und seines Textes*, in: *Arbeiten zur neutestamentlichen Textforschung* II, Berlin 1967, p. 81-90, see also ALAND, in: *NTS* 14 1965/66, p. 176-185, and J. DUPLACY, "Une Tâche importante en Difficulté: l'Édition du Nouveau Testament en Grec", in: *NTS* 14 1967/68, p. 457-468. See also E. C. COLWELL, I. A. SPARKS, F. WISSE, P. R. McREYNOLDS, "The International Greek New Testament Project: a Status Report", in: *JBL* 87 1968, p. 187-197.

[4] J. D. YODER, "Concordance to the Distinctive Greek Text of Codex Bezae", in: *NTS* II, Leiden 1961, see also J. D. YODER, "The Language of the Gospel Variants of Codex Bezae" in: *NT* 3 1959, p. 241-248 and J. D. YODER, "Semitisms in Codex Bezae, in: *JBL* 78 1959, p. 317-321.

CHAPTER ONE

SYRIA

a. THE DIATESSARON

In 1939 C. Peters brought together the results of the work by D. Plooy and A. Baumstark in a book entitled: *Das Diatessaron Tatians, seine Überlieferung und sein Nachwirken im Morgen- und Abendland sowie der heutige Stand seiner Erforschung* [1]. They had come to the conclusion that Tatian made use of a fifth source, the Gospel of the Hebrews, and that the Diatessaron had a great influence upon the early versions of the New Testament, in particular on the Old Syriac, the Old Latin, the Armenian and the Georgian version [2].

These results were far from generally accepted. In 1948 B. M. Metzger summed up the points of view in these words: "A still larger problem which continues to divide scholarly opinion is the extent of the alleged Tatianic influence upon the textual history of the Gospels—a problem which perhaps will never by satisfactorily settled" [3]. And more than ten years later L. Leloir, one of the connoiseurs of the Diatessaron, writes about the apocryphal element: "La proportion d'éléments apocryphes dans le Δ (sc. Diatessaron) n'est pourtant pas élévée, si bien qu'un évangile purement apocryphe n'a pu intervenir dans le rédaction du Δ que comme source occasionelle et secondaire" [4].

These sceptical remarks did not prevent the publishing of a number of very important editions of the Diatessaron. In 1951 the Persian Diatessaron appeared with an Italian translation. Messina, who published this text, had a keen eye for the importance of this

---

[1] C. PETERS, "Das Diatessaron Tatians, seine Überlieferung und sein Nachwirken in Morgen- und Abendland sowie der heutige Stand seiner Erforschung", in: *Orientalia Christiana Analecta* 123, Roma 1939.

[2] See KLIJN, *Survey*, p. 87-110.

[3] B. M. METZGER, "The Evidence of the Versions for the Text of the New Testament", in: M. M. PARVIS and A. P. WIKGREN, *New Testament Manuscript Studies*, Chicago 1948, p. 25-68, p. 29.

[4] L. LELOIR, "Le Diatessaron de Tatien", in: *L'Orient Syrien* I 1956, p. 208-231 and 313-334, p. 317. An excellent survey of work in the field of the Diatessaron by TJ. BAARDA, "Op Zoek naar de Tekst van het Diatessaron", in: *VT* 32 1961/62, p. 107-119.

text with its parallels with the Gospel of the Hebrews and the Protevangelium of James. However, the order of this Diatessaron is quite different from the other known Diatessara and this poses the question whether this text can be called a Diatessaron or whether it is a compilation of Old Syriac pericopes translated into Persian [1].

Two years later Leloir published a new edition and a translation of the Armenian version of Ephrem's commentary on the Diatessaron [2]. Again two years later after this, he was entrusted with the publication of the original Syriac text of this commentary [3]. Textual critics were already indebted to Leloir for these two works but he added to these a summary of quotations from the New Testament in the Syriac and the Armenian text of Ephrem's commentary with an apparatus of the readings in the Old Syriac translations, the Peshitto, the Armenian translation, quotations in Syriac and Armenian authors, the Latin translations and quota-

---

[1] G. MESSINA, "Lezioni Apocrifi del Diatessaron Persiano", in: *Bibl* 30 1949, p. 10-27 and IDEM, "Parallelismi Semitismi Lezioni tendenzioni nell' Armonia Persiano", in: *idem* 30 1949, p. 356-376; B. M. METZGER, "Tatian's Diatessaron and a Persian Harmony of the Gospels", in: *JBL* 69 1950, p. 261-280, see also IDEM, "Tatian's Diatessaron and a Persian Harmony of the Gospels", in: *Chapters in the History of New Testament Textual Criticism*, in: *NTTS* IV, Leiden 1963, p. 97-120; G. MESSINA, "Diatessaron Persiano", in: *BO* 14, Roma 1951, see *Review* by H. J. VOGELS, in *TL* 76 1951, c. 545-547; A. J. B. HIGGINGS, "The Persian Gospel Harmony as a Witness to Tatian's Diatessaron", in: *JTS* n. S. 3 1952, p. 83-87, and IDEM, "The Persian and Arabic Gospel Harmonies", in: *Studia Evangelica*, in: *TU* 73 1959, p. 793-810.

[2] L. LELOIR, "Saint Ephrem Commentaire de l'Évangile Concordant", in: *CSCO* 137, I Louvain 1953; 142, II Louvain 1954; L. MARIÈS, "Pour l'Étude du Diatessaron", in: *RSR* 44 1956, p. 228-233.

[3] L. LELOIR, "L'Original Syriaque du Commentaire de S. Éphrem sur le Diatessaron", in: *Bibl* 40 1959, p. 959-970, and IDEM, "Saint Éphrem, Commentaire de l'Évangile Concordant, Texte Syriaque (Manuscrit Chester Beatty 709)". Édité et Traduit par DOM LOUIS LELOIR, in: *Chester Beatty Monographs* No. 8, Dublin 1963, see also J. N. BIRDSALL, "The Syriac Original of the Commentary of Ephrem the Syrian upon the Concordant Gospel", in: *The Evangelical Quarterly* 37 1965, p. 132-141. Comparison of the Syriac and Armenian text in L. LELOIR, "Divergences entre l'Original Syriaque et la Version Arménienne du Commentaire d'Éphrem sur le Diatessaron", in: *Mélanges Eugène Tisserant*, in: *Studi e Testi* 232, Città del Vaticano 1964, p. 303-331. For fragments of the Commentary in Syriac, see TJ. BAARDA, "A Syriac Fragment of Mar Ephraem's Commentary on the Diatessaron", in: *NTS* 8 1961/62, p. 287-300, with an addition by L. ABRAMOWSKI-A. F. GOODMAN, "Luke XIII. 46 ΠΑΡΑΤΙΘΕΜΑΙ in a rare Syriac rendering", in: *idem* 13 1966/67, p. 290-291, see also P. ORTIZ VALDIVIELSO, "Un nuevo fragmento siríaco del Commentario de S. Efrén al Diatessaron (P. Palau Rib. 2)", in: *Studia Papyrol.* 5 1966, p. 7-17.

tions in Latin authors [1]. Finally Leloir published a French translation based upon both the Armenian and the Syriac text [2].

To all this we may add a collection of quotations from the Diatessaron in early Syriac ecclesiastical authors brought together by Ortiz de Urbina [3] and two parts of the edition of the Liège Diatessaron by Dr. A. H. A. Bakker [4].

But is seemed as if all these important publications did not affect the general attitude towards the value of the Diatessaron. We may quote the words of Leloir again as found in his latest work: "Il n'est pas possible, dans l'état actuel de nos connaissances, de déterminer avec une absolue certitude si le Diatessaron a été écrit en Orient ou en Occident, si la langue dans laquelle il est écrit a été le syriaque ou le grec. Pourtant, l'origine syriaque paraît plus probable" [5]. This conclusion is in agreement with what can be found in the textbooks. Metzger even deals with the Diatessaron in his chapter on "Patristic Quotations", but he concludes: "It is doubtless true, however, that not a few instances of harmonisation of the text of the Gospels in certain witnesses (notably the Western witnesses) are to be ascribed to Tatian's influence" [6].

Now quite unexpectedly the text of the Diatessaron has become the centre of interest since the discovery that this text shows a large measure of agreement with the Gospel of Thomas, one of the writings discovered in Nag Hammadi.

Already before the official publication of the text [7] Quispel had noticed the agreement between a number of *logia* in the Gospel

---

[1] L. LELOIR, "Témoignage d'Éphrem sur le Diatessaron", in: *CSCO* 227, Subsidia 19, Louvain 1962, see also L. LELOIR, "L'Évangile d'Éphrem d'après les Oeuvres éditées. Recueil des Textes", in: *idem* 180, Subsidia 12, Louvain 1958.

[2] *Éphrem de Nisibe*, "Commentaire de l'Évangile concordant ou Diatessaron. Traduit du Syriaque et de l'Arménienne", par L. LELOIR, in: *Sourc. Chrét.* 121, Paris 1966.

[3] *Biblia Polyglotta Matritensia*, Series VI: "Vetus Evangelium Syrorum et exinde excerptum Diatessaron Tatiani", editionem curavit IGNATIUS ORTIZ DE URBINA, Matriti 1967.

[4] "The Liège Diatessaron . . ." by † D. PLOOY and † C. A. PHILLIPS, A. H. A. BAKKER . . ., Part VI and VII, in: *Verhandel. der Kon. Nederl. Akad. van Wetensch.*, afd. Letterk., nieuwe Reeks, deel XXXI, Amsterdam 1963 and 1965.

[5] LELOIR, "Éphrem", in: *Sourc. Chrét.*, p. 18.

[6] METZGER, *Text*, p. 92.

[7] A. GUILLAUMONT, H.-CH. PUECH, G. QUISPEL, W. TILL and †YASSAH ʿABD AL MASIH, *The Gospel according to Thomas, Coptic Text established and translated*, Leiden-London 1959 (also in Dutch and French editions).

of Thomas, the Diatessaron, the quotations in the Ps. Clementines, fragments of Jewish Christian Gospels and quotations in the work of Justin Martyr. In an article written in 1957 Quispel stated his opinion which has hardly changed during the twelve years following[1]. It amounts to this: Tatian used a fifth source, a Jewish-Christian Gospel[2], in composing his Diatessaron, which source was also known to Justin and the Ps. Clementines and which influenced the Western Text.

These important conclusions—not only for the Diatessaron but also for the Western Text as a whole—have to be critically reviewed. We may follow up five lines of appoach:

1. *The Text of the Logia in the Gospel of Thomas and the Text of the Diatessaron*

The many agreements between the Logia of the synoptic type in the Gospel of Thomas and the text of the Diatessaron proves that in Syria, where the Gospel of Thomas was written, a particular text of the New Testament existed[3].

To this general statement we may add a few remarks. The parallels between Ev. Th. and the Diatessara can be explained in several ways. The Diatessaron might depend on the Ev. Th., but this seems improbable, because the parallels are limited to

---

[1] G. QUISPEL, "The Gospel of Thomas and the New Testament", in: *VC* 11 1957, p. 189-207, cf. G. QUISPEL, "The Diatessaron and the Historical Jesus", in: *Studi e Materiali di Storia nelle Religioni* 38 1967, p. 463-472. He apparently found a faithful follower in M. MEES, "Die Änderungen und Zusätze im Matthäus-Evangelium des Codex Bezae", in: *Vetera Christianorum* 4 1967, p. 107-129.

[2] Quispel's ideas about the Jewish-Christian Gospels are not clear. Usually he speaks about a Gospel of the Hebrews, but in one of his latest publications he refers to the " 'Gospel of the Hebrews' (Nazarenes)". This curious title is probably intended to say that, according to Quispel, some relation exists between the Gospel of the Hebrews and the Gospel of the Nazarenes. But what relation? In his article mentioned in the preceeding note he says, p. 191: ". . . the Nazarene Gospel and the Ebionite Gospel were just recensions of an underlying Gospel of the Hebrews". This is repeated in his "L'Évangile selon Thomas et le Diatessaron", in: *VC* 1959, p. 87-117, p. 116, n. 2, where it is said that the Gospel of the Hebrews is "d'origine araméenne". But in 1967 Quispel writes in his "Makarius, das Thomas-evangelium und das Lied von der Perle", in: *Supplem. to NT* XV 1967, p. 81, contrary to his earlier statements: "Es ist naheliegend, das *Hebräerevangelium* für eine erweiternde Übersetzung des *Nazaräerevangeliums* zu halten".

[3] See QUISPEL, *Diatessaron*, p. 89-95, and R. SCHIPPERS, *Het Evangelie van Thomas*, Kampen 1960, with a contribution by TJ. BAARDA giving a very useful list of witnesses supporting variant readings in Ev. Th.

those of the synoptic type in the Ev. Th. The Ev. Th. might depend
on the Diatessaron and this is less improbable though it means
that the Ev. Th. must have been written at the end of the second
century [1]. This seems rather late. A third possibility is the dependence of both Ev. Th. and Diatessaron on a similar text of the
Gospel. This might be a canonical Gospel or an Apocryphal Gospel.
Quispel gives some parallels between Ev. Th. and Diatessaron
which would show that the two writings are dependent on the same
extra-canonical text [2]. These are:

Matth. 5, 11: ... καὶ διώξωσιν ...
Luk. 6, 22: ... μισήσωσιν ...
Ev. Th. 68: ... when you are hated and persecuted ...
Tᵃ l ᵗ: ... hate and persecute ...
Ps. Clem. *Hom.* XI 20 2: ... χωρίζοντες, διώκοντες, μισοῦντες.
　　　　　　XII 29 4: ... διωκόμενοι, μισούμενοι, λοιδορού-
　　　　　　　　　　μενοι
Polyc., *ad Phil.* 12, 3: ... *pro prosequentibus et odientibus.*

Both the Ev. Th. and Diatessaron seem to harmonise Matthew
and Luke. It appears that this harmonisation is already present
in Polycarp and the Ps. Clementines. These last two writings might
be using independent Gospel-tradition. But even if they did in
these passages, it appears to be absolutely unnecessary to suppose
that for this reason Ev. Th. and Diatessaron are using the same or a
similar independent source. Harmonising Matthew and Luke seems
to be an obvious procedure for Tatian in this passage.

In Ev. Th. 33 we find an interesting parallel with T[1] which reads:

T[1]	Ev. Th.
No one sets a light,	for no one lights a lamp
when it is kindled, under	and puts it under
the cornvat, nor under the bed,	a bushel, nor does he put it
nor in a hidden place,	in a hidden place,
but one sets it on the	but he sets it on a
candlestick, that it may	lampstand, so that all who
light all those that are	go in and out may see the light.
in the house [3].	

---

[1] So BAARDA, in: SCHIPPERS, *Het Evangelie van Thomas,* p. 155.

[2] See QUISPEL, *Diatessaron,* p. 111-114.

[3] Nimen en sett dat licht alst ontfinct es onder dat corenvat noch onder
dat bedde noch in ene verborgene stat mar op den candelere so sett ment
opdatt lichten sole allen den ghenen die int hus syn.

Quispel supposes that the text in the Diatessaron can be explained from a text like that in Ev. Th. The only thing which Tatian had to do was to add part of Mark 4, 21 (under the bed) and adapt the end to the text of Matth. 5, 14.

A close look at the text, however, shows that we are dealing with two quite different traditions which can be traced back to different Gospels. T¹ consists of two parts. The first part is the result of a harmonisation of Luk. 8, 16 and Luk. 11, 33. This is apparently the original text of the Diatessaron because the same harmonisation can be found in Aphraates I 24 19-22. The second part has been taken from Matth. 5, 15 [1].

The text of Ev. Th. appears to be almost identical with Luk. 11, 33 as it is rendered in sy^c. Here we find:

ܠܐ ܐܢܫ ܡܢܝܪ ܫܪܓܐ
ܘܣܐܡ ܠܗ ܬܚܘܬ
ܘܠܐܬܐ ܐܘ ܒܐܬܪܐ ܟܣܝܐ .
ܐܠܐ ܣܐܡ ܠܗ ܠܥܠ ܡܢ
ܡܢܪܬܐ ܕܐܝܠܝܢ ܕܥܠܝܢ
ܚܙܝܢ ܢܘܗܪܗ

The only deviation is the reading "nor does he put" l. ܐܘ (or). The end of the passage in Ev. Th. must be a free rendering by the author of this Gospel.

Now that we have been able to point to two different traditions from which the passages in the Diatessaron and Ev. Th. can be explained, it is impossible to suppose mutual dependence. Matters are much more complicated but also much more interesting. We might even suggest that the text in Ev. Th. and in sy^c was present in a pre-Diatessaron text of the Gospel in Syria.

Finally Quispel points to Ev. Th. 57 and T¹. In Ev. Th. a parallel is found with Matth. 13, 25. It shows some deviations from the accepted text which are in agreement with T¹:

It is said that the enemy comes "during the night" l. ἐν τῷ καθεύδειν. Next we find:
he sowed l. ἐπέσπειρεν cum D e k q sy^scp sa bo Ir T^a
seed l. τοῦ σίτου cum Titus of Bostra.

---

[1] See PLOOY, *Liège Diatessaron*, p. 67.

Undoubtedly these readings are interesting, but we do not see any reason to explain them from an uncanonical text. The source could have been any text of the canonical Gospels.

From these examples it appears that agreement between the Diatessaron and the Ev. Th., whether supported by other witnesses or not, can never be explained from a common use of extra-canonical matter, since it remains possible and it is even conceivable that these writings which originated in the same region, quoted from the same canonical text of the Gospels, a text which many peculiar readings.

The readings Quispel has shown are interesting in so far as they show a curious text of the Gospels in Syria.

2. The Text of the Logia in the Gospel of Thomas and the Quotations in the Ps. Clementines and Justin Martyr

The significance of the agreement between these writings is that most scholars agree that both the Ps. Clementines and Justin Martyr quoted from an extra-canonical Gospel tradition. But, as far as we know, it is also true that nobody likes to go so far as to say that these writings show extra-canonical matter only [1].

For this reason Quispel is making a methodological mistake when he states that those instances where the Ev. Th. agrees with the Ps. Clementines, have been taken from a Jewish-Christian Gospel [2]. This opinion overlooks the difficulty of differentiations between those quotations in the Ps. Clementines which have been taken from the canonical Gospels and those which come from other sources.

It was Strecker who tried to find a rule by which we might decide which quotations were taken from extra-canonical sources. This rule reads [3]:

a) The main variants in a quotation must be available, literally of almost literally, in a non-Clementine text, but it has to be assumed that the one text does not depend upon the other.

---

[1] See for quotations in Ps. Clementines G. STRECKER, "Das Judenchristentum in den Pseudoklementinen", in: *TU* 70 1958, p. 117-136, and in Justin Martyr E. MASSAUX, "Le Texte du Sermon sur la Montagne de Matthieu utilisé par Saint Justin", in: *Ephem. Theol. Lovanienses* 28 1952, p. 411-448, and A. BELLINZONI, "The Sayings of Jesus in the Writings of Justin Martyr", in: *Supplem. to NT* XVII 1967, who both, however, contrary to many former studies, arrived at the conclusion that Justin used the canonical Gospels.

[2] QUISPEL, *New Testament*, p. 190.

[3] STRECKER, *o.c.*, p. 130.

b) The variants in a quotation must not occur in any canonical text and it has to be assumed that the author of the Ps. Clementines is not responsible for this form of the text himself.

If we apply this rule the result usually will be that only *agrapha* can be accepted as being taken from extra-canonical sources.

It is of course wise that Strecker keeps on the safe side. But still we doubt whether his rule is as safe as it appears to be. The decision whether a passage is canonical or not depends inter alia upon the presence or absence of the passages in our canonical Gospels. This rule could only be applied safely if we knew all the canonical texts. It is possible at any time that a hitherto unknown parallel between the Ps. Clementines and a canonical text may be discovered. At the same time Strecker has to decide that the passage or the reading is no longer extra-canonical. On the other hand Strecker seems to exclude the possibility that both a canonical text and the Ps. Clementines were independently influenced by extra-canonical matter.

From this we see how difficult it is to decide what is canonical and what is extra-canonical. For this reason we abstain from giving general rules and go into some examples given by Quispel [1]:

I. *Rec. Syr.* III 14 7 and Ev. Th. 9: on the road 1. παρὰ τὴν ὁδόν in Matth. 13, 4, Mark 4, 4 and Luk. 8, 5, but ἐπὶ 1. παρὰ (Mark) cum 7 28 33 827 1241 and (Luke) cum R Tᵉ [a]. Quispel supposes an original על אורחא, but it seems unnecessary because harmonisation with the following verse is obvious [2].

: 2. *Rec. Lat.* VI 13 5: *si illi mutuo dant his qui habent unde reddant, nos etiam his demus a quibus recipere non speramus.*

Hom. XI 32 I: ἐὰν ὁ ἐν πλάνη δανίζῃ τοῖς ἔχουσιν, ἡμεῖς καὶ τοῖς μὴ ἔχουσιν.

Ev. Th. 95: If you have money do not lend at interest but give (them) to him from whom you will not receive them (back).

Luk. 6, 34: καὶ ἐὰν δανείσητε παρ' ὧν ἐλπίζετε λαβεῖν . . .

Luk. 6, 35: καὶ δανείζετε μηδὲν ἀπελπίζοντες.

We notice an agreement in *Rec.* and Ev. Th., since both show the word "to give", but cf. *da* 1. δανείζετε in Tᵖ and *his qui non*

---

[1] G. QUISPEL, "L'Évangile selon Thomas et les Clémentines", in: *VC* 12 1958, p. 181-196, p. 183-191.

[2] How obvious appears from W. BAUER, *Gr.-Deutsches Wörterbuch*, Berlin 1952, p. VIII: ". . . dass ihre Saatkörner unter die Dornen oder auf den Weg gefallen sind".

habent l. μηδὲν ἀπελπίζοντες cum r¹ and *et si mutuum dederint alii. . .* in Tᵃ. Quispel supposes that Ev. Th. makes the laws found in Ex. 22, 25, Lev. 25, 36-37 and Deut. 23, 19-20, stricter. There it is only said that one is not allowed to give money on interest to a compatriot. Here we find that one has to give without expecting anything back.

3. *Rec. Syr.* II 3 5: μὴ μαργαρίτας τοῖς χοίροις προβάλλωμεν [1].

Ev. Th. 93: Throw not the pearls to the swine.

Cf. Matth. 7, 6: μαργαρίτας l. μαργαρίτας ὑμῶν cum syᶜ ᵖᵃˡ Tᵛ Chr., Basil. and τοῖς χοίροις l. ἔμπροσθεν τῶν χοίρων cum Tert.

These variants can only prove that somewhere a text existed deviating from the text we accept in our modern editions.

4. *Hom.* VIII 22 4: εἰς τὸ θεοῦ δεῖπνον.

Rec. Lat. IV 35 5: . . . *ad coenam* . . .

Ev. Th. 64: . . . he had prepared the dinner (δεῖπνον) . . .

Quispel points to Matth. 22, 1-4 where there is spoken of γάμοι. The deviation he explains from an original מישׁתותא. It seems more likely that Ev. Th. knew Luk. 14, 16-24.

5. *Hom.* III 67 1: ὡς πόλιν ἐν ὕψει ᾠκοδομημένην.

Ev. Th. 22: A city built on a high mountain (and) fortified.

Pap. Ox. I: πόλις ᾠκοδομημένη ἐπ᾽ ἄκρον ὄρους ὑψηλοῦ καὶ ἐστηριγμένη.

Matth. 5, 14: . . . πόλις . . . ἐπάνω ὄρους κειμένη.

The reading "built" is known from sy ˢᶜᵖ Tᵃ Aug Hil, and "fortified" we also find in Tᵖ. The variants are interesting, but we can only repeat what we said in 3.

6. *Hom.* III 52 1: ὁ πατὴρ ὁ οὐράνιος.

Ev. Th. 40: . . . without the Father . . .

Matth. 15, 13: ὁ πατήρ μου ὁ οὐράνιος.

Cf. om. μου in ff² and Ephrem.

om. ὁ οὐράνιος in Cypr.

It is far-fetched to suppose a basic אבא. In Matthew we meet πατήρ with and without μου (18, 35 and 23, 9).

7. *Rec. Syr.* II 26 6: οὐκ ἦλθον βαλεῖν εἰρήνην ἐπὶ τὴν γῆν ἀλλὰ πόλεμον (ܘܩܪܒܐ).

Ev. Th. 16: Men possibly think that I have come to throw peace upon the world (κόσμος) . . . I have come to throw divisions upon the earth, fire, sword, war (πόλεμος).

---

[1] Quispel uses the Greek text of the Syriac translated by W. FRANKENBERG, "Die Syrischen Clementinen mit Griechischen Paralleltext", in: *TU* 48, 3 1937.

Matth. 10, 34: μὴ νομίσητε ὅτι ἦλθον βαλεῖν εἰρήνην ἐπὶ τὴν γῆν·
οὐκ ἦλθον βαλεῖν εἰρήνην ἀλλὰ μάχαιραν.

Luk. 12, 51: δοκεῖτε ὅτι εἰρήνην παρεγενομένην δοῦναι ἐν τῇ γῇ;
οὐχί, λέγω ὑμῖν, ἀλλ' ἢ διαμερισμόν.

Quispel explains the word πόλεμος in *Rec.* and *Ev. Th.* from an
original ܣܝܦܐ being both "war" and "sword" in Syriac. But this
possibility in the Syriac language does not imply "une tradition,
d'origine araméenne, qui ne s'identifie pas avec Q" [1].

8. *Ev. Th.* 39: The Pharisees and the Scribes have received the
keys of knowledge, they have hidden them. They did not enter and
they did not let those (enter) who wished.

Matth. 23, 13: Οὐαὶ δὲ ὑμῖν, γραμματεῖς καὶ φαρισαῖοι, ὑποκριταί,
ὅτι κλείετε τὴν βασιλείαν τῶν οὐρανῶν ἔμπροσθεν τῶν ἀνθρώπων·
ὑμεῖς γὰρ οὐκ εἰσέρχεσθε, οὐδὲ τοὺς εἰσερχομένους ἀφίετε εἰσελθεῖν.

Luk. 11, 52: Οὐαὶ ὑμῖν τοῖς νομικοῖς, ὅτι ἤρατε τὴν κλεῖδα τῆς
γνώσεως· αὐτοὶ οὐκ εἰσήλθατε καὶ τοὺς εἰσερχομένους ἐκωλύσατε.

Cf. The Pharisees and the Scribes l. γραμματεῖς καὶ φαρισαῖοι
(Matth.) and τοῖς νομικοῖς (Luk.) in Luk. 11, 53 in D lat.

have received l. ἤρατε (Luk.) cum 1604, cf. *Rec. Syr.* I 54 7:

ܡܚܕܐ ܕܝܕܥܬܐ

the keys l. τὴν κλεῖδα (Luk.) cum Just q sy^sc T^p e a.

add. they have hidden them, cf. Θ: ἐκρύψατε ἤρατε and ἐκρύψατε
l. ἤρατε cum D 157 lat sy ^sc T^e a.

and who wished to enter l. τοὺς εἰσερχομένους (Matth. and Luk.)
cum *Hom.* III 18 3, cf. in Matth. βουλομένους l. εἰσερχομένους cum
1093.

Quispel explains the variant reading λαμβάνειν and αἴρειν from
the Syriac word ܫܩܠ. This Syriac word, like the Aramaic equivalent
שקל can be translated by both words. Quispel, however, rightly
supposes that an original קבל is more in agreement with the con-
text. But this can not be translated "to take away". For this
reason Quispel writes: "il n'est pas absolument exclu que קבל ait
déja remplacé שקל dans une source, orale ou écrite, araméenne" [2].
We may relegate this remark to the realm of imagination.

9. *Rec. Syr.* and *Lat.* II 28 3 and *Ev. Th.* 54 read the words
"kingdom of Heaven" l. "Kingdom of God" in Luk. 6. 28. This
kind of variant reading is quite common in textual tradition.

10. *Rec. Lat.* III 62 2 quotes Matth. 13, 45. It is said with *Ev. Th.*

---

[1] QUISPEL, *Clémentines*, p. 189.
[2] QUISPEL, *Clémentines*, p. 190.

76 that the merchant was "prudent". This variant reading is also to be found in the Biography of Rabula.

These examples are very interesting. They show some peculiar readings found in a number of writings which are all of them related with Antioch or Edessa. But none of these variant readings need be explained by extra-canonical influence. They are readily explained by a particular Gospel text in Syria.

We may add to this list four passages where Strecker and Quispel agree that we are dealing with extra-canonical material.

1. [1] *Hom.* XVIII 1 3 = XVIII 3 4: ὁ γὰρ ἀγαθὸς εἷς ἐστιν, ὁ πατὴρ ὁ ἐν τοῖς οὐρανοῖς (III 57 and XVII 4 2 om. ὁ γὰρ ἀγαθὸς εἷς ἐστιν).
Just., *Dial.* 101 2: εἷς ἐστιν ἀγαθός, ὁ πατήρ μου ὁ ἐν τοῖς οὐρανοῖς.
Matth. 19, 17: εἷς ἐστιν ὁ ἀγαθός.
Cf. Ephrem, *Comment. Diat.* XV 9: Un seul est bon, le Père, qui est au ciel. See also Marcosians in Iren. I 20 2.

2. [2] *Hom.* III 57 1: γίνεσθε ἀγαθοὶ καὶ οἰκτίρμονες ὡς ὁ πατὴρ ὁ ἐν τοῖς οὐρανοῖς ὃς ἀνατέλλει τὸν ἥλιον ἐπ' ἀγαθοῖς καὶ πονηροῖς καὶ φέρει τὸν ὑετὸν ἐπὶ δικαίοις καὶ ἀδίκοις.

We find Luk. 6, 36 together with Matth. 5, 45. The same we find in Just., *Apol.* I 15 13 and *Dial.* 96 3. We have the following variant readings in *Hom.* and Justin from Luk. 6, 36:
ἀγαθοὶ (Just. χρηστοὶ) καὶ οἰκτίρμονες 1. οἰκτίρμονες
ὡς 1. καθώς cum Just. *Hom.* 700 Or Did Ath Chr
ὁ πατὴρ ἐν τ. οὐρ. (*Hom.*) and ὁ πατ. ὑμῶν ὁ οὐράνιος (Just. *Dial.*)
1. ὁ πατὴρ ὑμῶν cf., however, ℵ𝑐 483 954 Bas.
ὃς 1. ὅτι (Justin partic.) cum 372 latsy T[1] Or Ir Tert Hil
ἐπὶ πον. κ. ἀγαθ. (*Hom.*) 1. ∞ cum latsy sa Or Tert T[1].

We can compare φέρει τὸν ὑετὸν with T[1]: "and makes his rain fall", Aphraates and the Syriac version: ܘܡܚܬ ܡܛܪܐ. This may be the second part of the reading beginning with "His sun let shine" as in T[1] sy and Aphr.

3. [3] *Hom.* XVIII 4 2 and Just., *Apol.* I 63 3: οὐδεὶς ἔγνω τὸν πατέρα εἰ μὴ ὁ υἱός, cf. Matth. 11, 27. The variant reading ἔγνω 1. ἐπιγινώσκω and τὸν πατ. ... υἱός 1. ∞ can be found in ecclesiastical authors.

4. Finally we add the reading only found in Strecker [4]. Both

---

[1] QUISPEL, *Diatessaron*, p. 100 and STRECKER, *o.c.*, p. 131.

[2] QUISPEL, *Diatessaron*, p. 99, and STRECKER, *o.c.*, p. 131, but a survey of the entire attestation in BELLINZONI, *o.c.*, p. 8-14.

[3] QUISPEL, *Diatessaron*, p. 99-100, and STRECKER, *o.c.*, p. 132, see again Bellinzoni, *o.c.*, p. 25-28.

[4] STRECKER, *o.c.*, p. 133, and BELLINZONI, *o.c.*, p. 114-116.

Hom. XIX 2 5 and Just., *Dial.* 76 5 have put together Matth. 25, 30 and 25, 41: ὑπάγετε εἰς τὸ σκότος τὸ ἐξώτερον, ὃ ἡτοίμασεν ὁ πατὴρ τῷ διαβόλῳ καὶ τοῖς ἀγγέλοις αὐτοῦ.

The second part shows some agreement with 25, 41 in D fam. 1 22 it Ir: ὁ ἡτοίμασεν ὁ πατήρ μου.

Not all these examples are interesting for textual criticism. The third one might have been taken from an extra-canonical source, but this source probably did not influence the text of the Gospels. Numbers 2 and 4 are very interesting because here passages have been put together by different authors in the same way. This can hardly have come about accidentally. They might have been circulating in this way outside the canonical text, but ultimately it seems probable that the passages originated from the canonical Gospels.

It is this harmonising material which we continuously meet from the time of the Apostolic Fathers onward. Recent investigators like Strecker, Köster [1] and Bellinzoni agree that this material might have been known in an oral form, but that it has come down from canonical Gospels. The variant readings which agree with manuscripts known to us might have already been available in the canonical text of that time, but it is also possible that the oral tradition in its turn influenced the canonical text.

3. *The supposed Semitic influence in the Gospel of Thomas and the Witnesses to the Western Text*

The explanation of variant readings from a supposed Semitic original has been widely applied. Modern research in this field goes back to A. J. Wensinck and has been continued by M. Black [2]. The evaluation of these variant readings appears to be difficult. Black says that in " 'the Bezan redaction' more of the primitive 'Aramaized' Greek text has been left unrevised than in the redaction . . . by the Vatican and Sinaitic Uncials". This would mean that variant readings which show Semitic idiom have a serious claim to be original. But Black says on the same page that in particular "the Old Syriac has been influenced at its source by an extra-canonical and apocryphal Gospel tradition of the sayings

---

[1] H. Köster, "Synoptische Überlieferung bei den apostolischen Vätern", in: *TU* 65 1957.
[2] See Klijn, *Survey*, p. 146-150.

of Jesus . . ." [1]. This means that Semitic idiom points to a secondary text, being influenced by and outside-source. Who is able to decide on the question whether we are dealing with a "primitive 'Aramaized' Greek text" or with a reading that "has been influenced . . . by an extra-canonical . . . Gospel tradition" ? An other difficulty is that we cannot always say whether we are dealing with Aramaisms or the influence of the Syriac language.

In the list given under b. we have pointed to the difficulties with regard to the supposed influence of an Aramaic original in the examples 1, 4, 6, 7, and 8. In addition Quispel gives another group of about 13 cases where the "tradition araméenne" would be visible [2]. We may say that there are none of these which can not be explained from the Syriac [3].

How careful we have to be can be shown by one striking example. Guillaumont points to the reading in Pap. Ox 1: νηστεύειν τὸν κόσμον [4]. This reading is unusual in Greek. The parallel in Ev. Th. 27 reads: επκοϲⲙοϲ, translated by Guillaumont: ἀπὸ τοῦ κόσμου.

Guillaumont shows that both τὸν κόσμον and ἀπὸ τοῦ κόσμου can be found in Liber Graduum. This means that in Syria the *logion* circulated in the form it is met with in the Coptic and in the Greek version of Ev. Th. Guillaumont accepts that the more difficult reading in the Greek version is the oldest one. He supposed an original Aramaic לעלמא but adds: "Nous n'avons pas d'autre exemple à alléguer avec un complément; mais elle nous paraît tout à fait possible" [5]. The retranslation into Aramaic is purely guess-work! But Quispel says: "Guillaumont führt das (sc. τὸν κόσμον) zurück auf den aramäischen Ausdruck צום ל 'fasten von' ". And he goes on: "Daraus muß man schließen, daß das *Thomasevangelium* eine aramäische Quelle benutzt hat". [6] A less probable argument for an Aramaic source is hardly possible to imagine.

---

[1] M. BLACK, *An Aramaic Approach to the Gospels and Acts*, Oxford 1967³, p. 279.

[2] QUISPEL, *Diatessaron*, p. 115.

[3] Cf. BAARDA, in: SCHIPPERS, *o.c.*, p. 155: "Het is ons namelijk gebleken dat de tekst van de Koptische Thomas niet teruggaat op een (West-)Aramees, maar een Syrisch exemplaar".

[4] A. GUILLAUMONT, "ΝΗΣΤΕΥΕΙΝ ΤΟΝ ΚΟΣΜΟΝ", in: *Bulletin de L'Institut Français d'Archéologie Orientale* 61 1962, p. 15-23.

[5] GUILLAUMONT, *art. c.*, p. 21.

[6] QUISPEL, *Makarius*, p. 21.

4. *The Agreement between the Gospel of Thomas and Witnesses to the Western Text*

Quispel has drawn up a very interesting list with readings found both in the Ev. Th. and the witnesses of the Western Text [1]. None of these can claim to prove extra-canonical influence on the text of the Ev. Th. or the Western witnesses. These variant readings only prove that the text in some Western witnesses was known in Syria, something we knew already from the Diatessaron.

6. *The Agreement between available extra-canonical Gospel Tradition and the Text of the New Testament*

Up to now we have failed to discover any trace of direct influence by extra-canonical tradition on the text of the New Testament. We do not say that it is not possible in the cases we dealt with, but that we have no way to prove it. There are two reasons for our failure. We have an imperfect knowledge of the oldest text in regions where the influence of extra-canonical material on the text can be supposed, and we have an equally imperfect knowledge of the extra-canonical matter itself. For this reason we must now go into the small bits of evidence of what is left of this extra-canonical matter.

This is available in some fragments of Jewish Christian Gospels. We give a list of those passages which show agreement with the canonical text of the New Testament. They are found in Hennecke, where Vielhauer splits up the fragments into three groups, those drawn from

The Gospel of the Nazarenes. Originally written in Aramaic or Syriac in the first half of the second century. Used in the environment of Beroea. Secondary to Matthew.

The Gospel of the Ebionites. Written in Greek at the beginning

---

[1] G. Quispel, "L'Évangile selon Thomas et le 'Texte Occidentale' du Nouveau Testament", in: *VC* 14 1960, p. 204-215. In the list we find 84 variant readings supported by Western witnesses. It is striking that 27 of them are supported by sa and bo. This strikingly agrees with the results gained by K. H. Kuhn, "Some Observations on the Coptic Gospel according to Thomas", in: *Le Muséon* 73 1960, p. 317-323, and W. Schrage, "Das Verhältnis des Thomas-Evangeliums zur synoptischen Tradition und zu den koptischen Evangelienübersetzungen", in: *Beih. ZNW* 29 1964. This work clearly shows that the Coptic Ev. Th. was influenced by the Coptic translation of the New Testament. See also *Reviews* by A. F. J. Klijn, in: *NT* 7 1965, p. 329-330, H. Quecke, in: *Le Muséon* 78 1965, p. 234-239, and R. McL. Wilson, in: *VC* 20 1966, p. 118-123.

of the second century. Used in the region East of the Jordan. Secondary to Matthew and Luke.

The Gospel of the Hebrews. Written in Greek at the beginning of the second century in Egypt. The relation with the canonical Gospels is hard to determine.

From the available fragments Vielhauer ascribes 36 fragments to the Gospel of the Nazarenes, 7 to the Gospel of the Hebrew and 7 to the Gospels of the Ebionites [1].

The main difficulty in evaluating the agreement between the fragments and the canonical text of the Gospels is our realisation that the Jewish-Christian Gospels apparently used one or more of the canonical Gospels.

1. Epiphanius, *Pan.* 30 12 4 [2]: καὶ τὸ βρῶμα αὐτοῦ μέλι ἄγριον οὗ ἡ γεῦσις ἡ τοῦ μάννα, ὡς ἐγκρὶς ἐν ἐλαίῳ.

This passage shows agreement with the text of Mark 1, 4 in T^a.

2. Epiphanius, *Pan.* 30 13 7-8 [3]: The passage speaks about the baptism of Jesus in which it is said: τὸ πνεῦμα τὸ ἅγιον ἐν εἴδει περιστερᾶς l. τὸ πνεῦμα ὡς περιστερὰν (Mark 1, 10, cf. Matth. 3, 16: ὡσεὶ περιστεράν and Luk. 3, 22), cum Just., *Dial* 88 4 and 8 and sy^s. Next we find ἐγὼ σήμερον γεγέννηκά σε l. οὗτός ἐστιν ... ὁ ἀγαπητός cum D a b c ff² l Just., *Dial.* 88 8, Clem Or in Luk. 3, 22. Finally: καὶ εὐθὺς περιέλαμψε τὸν τόπον φῶς μέγα, cf. Just., *Dial.* 88 3: καὶ πῦρ ἀνήφθη ἐν τῷ Ἰορδάνῃ; a g¹: *et cum baptizeretur* (g¹ add. *Iesus*) *lumen ingens* (g¹ *magnum*) *circumfulsit* (g¹ *fulgebat*) *de aqua* ... and T^e Ischo^{c}dad, Barsalibi, Ps. Cypr., *de Rebapt.* 17.

3. Jerome, *Contra Pel.* III 2 [4]: ... *quid peccavi, ut vadam et baptizer ab eo* ..., cf. Ev. Th. 104: which then is the sin that I have committed ... [5].

4. Jerome, *Comment. in Is.* 11, 2 [6]: *Factum est autem cum ascendisset Dominus de aqua, descendit fons omnis Spiritus Sancti, et requievit super eum, et dixit illi: Fili me, in omnibus Prophetis expectabant te, ut veniam et requiescam in te* ..., cf. Ephrem, *Comment. Diat* IV 3:

---

[1] P. VIELHAUER, "Judenchristliche Evangelien", in: HENNECKE-SCHNEEMELCHER, *Neutestamentliche Apokryphen* Band I, Tübingen, p. 75-108.

[2] VIELHAUER, *o.c.*, p. 103: Gospel of the Ebionites.

[3] VIELHAUER, *o.c.*, p. 103: Gospel of the Ebionites.

[4] VIELHAUER, *o.c.*, p. 95: Gospel of the Nazarenes. See also J. B. BAUER, "Sermo Peccati. Hieronymus und das Nazarenerevangelium", in: *BZ* n. F. 4 1963, p. 122-128.

[5] See QUISPEL, *New Testament*, p. 140, and E. HAENCHEN, "Literatur zum Thomasevangelium", in: *TR* 27 1961, p. 147-178 and 306-338, p. 164-165.

[6] VIELHAUER, *o.c.*, p. 107: Gospel of the Hebrews.

L'Esprit qui reposa sur lui pendant son baptême... L'Esprit descendit et se reposa que sur un seul ...

5. Cod. N.T. 566 ad Matth. 4, 5 [1]: ἐν Ἰερουσαλήμ l. εἰς τὴν ἁγίαν πόλιν cum T¹.

6. Cod. N.T. 1424 ad Matth. 5, 22 [2]: om. εἰκῆ cum permulti.

7. Cod. N.T. 1424 ad Matth. 11, 25 [3]: εὐχαριστῶ σοι

l. ἐξομολογοῦμαί σοι cum T¹ v e Marcion Tert (Luk. 10, 21).

8. Jerome, *Comment. in Matth.* 12, 13 [4]: *Caementarius eram manibus victum qua* ..., cf. T¹ (c. 87): so that he could not work with it [5].

9. Epiphanius, *Pan.* 30 14 5 [6]:

a) ἰδοὺ ἡ μήτηρ σου καὶ οἱ ἀδελφοί σου ἔξω ἑστήκασιν

b) τίς μού ἐστιν μήτηρ καὶ ἀδελφοί

c) καὶ ἐκτείνας τὴν χεῖρα ἐπὶ τοὺς μαθητὰς ἔφη

d) οὗτοί εἰσιν οἱ ἀδελφοί μου καὶ ἡ μήτηρ καὶ ἀδελφαὶ οἱ ποιοῦντες τὰ θελήματα [7] τοῦ πατρός μου.

Cf. for a) Luk. 8, 20: ἡ μήτηρ σου καὶ οἱ ἀδελφοί σου ἑστήκασιν ἔξω, but ἰδοὺ a. ἡ μήτηρ cum 999; ἔξω ἑστήκασιν I. ∽ cum D 213 c e Marcion Bas Acta Arch.[8]

Cf. for b) Matth. 12, 48 and Mark 3, 33: τίς ἐστιν ἡ μήτηρ μου καὶ (τίνες εἰσιν om. Mark) οἱ ἀδελφοί μου, but in Mark om. ἡ in 213 346 543 700 2145; om. μου¹ in W 291 700; om. μου² in B D arm.

Cf. for c) Matth. 12, 49: καὶ ἐκτείνας τὴν χεῖρα αὐτοῦ ἐπὶ τοὺς μαθητὰς αὐτοῦ εἶπεν, but om. αὐτοῦ p. χεῖρα cum D 1574 multi; om. αὐτοῦ² in Δ vg Chr; ἔφη l. εἶπεν cum 349 517 954 1675.

---

[1] VIELHAUER, *o.c.*, p. 95: Gospel of the Hebrews.
[2] VIELHAUER, *o.c.*, p. 96: Gospel of the Nazarenes.
[3] VIELHAUER, *o.c.*, p. 96: Gospel of the Nazarenes.
[4] VIELHAUER, *o.c.*, p. 96: Gospel of the Nazarenes.
[5] so dat hire nit met werken en mochte.
[6] VIELHAUER, *o.c.*, p. 103: Gospel of the Ebionites.
[7] The plural is in agreement with the words of "Our Father" in sy^s (Matth. 6, 10) and many Syriac Liturgies. See also L. E. WRIGHT, *Alterations of the Words of Jesus as quoted in the Litterature of the second Century*, Cambridge (Mass.) 1952, p. 92-93.
[8] See the interesting article by G. C. HANSON," Zu den Evangelienzitaten in den 'Acta Archelai' ", in: *Studia Patristica* VII, in: *TU* 92 1966, p. 473-485, with the conclusion, p. 484: "Das relativ geringe Material, das die aus manichäischen Quellen geschöpften Abschnitte der 'Acta Archelai' bieten, läßt doch den Schluß zu, daß nicht alle Spuren des Diatessaron, die in den Evangelienzitaten zu finden sind, erst auf den lateinischen Übersetzer und seine Vertrautheit mit seiner altlateinischen Bibel zurückgeht, sondern daß manche Tatianismen aus 'dem Evangelium', das die Manichäer benutzt haben, sich erhalten haben".

Cf. for d) Matth. 12, 50: ὅστις γὰρ ἂν ποιήσῃ τὸ θέλημα τοῦ πατρός μου τοῦ ἐν οὐρανοῖς, αὐτός μου ἀδελφὸς καὶ ἀδελφὴ καὶ μήτηρ and Luk. 8, 21: μήτηρ μου καὶ ἀδελφοί μου οὗτοί εἰσιν οἱ τὸν λόγον τοῦ Θεοῦ ἀκούοντες καὶ ποιοῦντες, but ἡ α. μήτηρ cum 597 multi; om. μου [1] 1 660 2145 b ff²; add οἱ α. ἀδελφοί cum multi [1].

10. Cod. N.T. 1424 ad Matth. 16, 2-3 [2]: om. verses cum multi.

11. Jerome, *Contra Pelag.* III 2: *Si peccavit frater tuus . . . septies in die . . .*, cf. Luk. 17, 4 and Matth. 18, 21-22. The same harmonisation of the two passages in Tᵉ [1].

12. Origen, *Comment. in Matth.* XV 14:

a) *Dixit . . . ad eum alter divitum: magister, quid bonum faciens vivam? Dixit ei: homo, legem et prophetas fac.*

b) *respondit ad eum: feci. Dixit ei: vade, vende omnia quae possides et divide pauperibus, et veni, sequere me . . .*

c) *Diliges proximum tuum sicut teipsum . . .*

d) *Simon, fili Ionae, facilius est camelum intrare per foramen acus quam divitem in regnum coelorum.*

Cf. for a) Matth. 19, 16-17, Mark. 10, 17-18 and Luk. 18, 18-19, but *dixit ad eum* l. αὐτῷ εἶπεν (Matth.) cum K C W alii, *dixit illi* in a; add. πλούσιος in Mark in A K M W Θ Π fam. 13 georg syʰᵐᵍ arm sa; τί ποιήσας in Matth. in ℵ L 28 33 157 and τί ποιῶν in Luk. in 1 131 209 a aur d f vg.

Cf. for b) Matth. 19, 20-21, Mark 10, 20-21 and Luke 18, 21-22, but ἀποκριθεὶς εἶπεν l. ἔφη (Mark) in K A D fam. 1 fam. 13 syˢ ᵖ and ἀποκριθεὶς ἔφη in C, cf. also *respondit ait* in aur b c f and *respondit dixit* in a ff² q f; *feci* l. ἐφυλαξάμην (Mark) in fam. 1 565 syˢ georg arm; *omnia quae possides* l. σου τὰ ὑπάρχοντα (Matth.) in f ff¹ syˢ; *divide* l. δὸς (Mark) in k a and fam. 13; om. καὶ ἕξεις . . . οὐρανοῖς (Matth.) in syˢ.

Cf. for d) Matth. 19, 24, Mark 10, 25 and Luk. 18, 25, but *in regnum coelorum* l. εἰς τὴν βασιλείαν τοῦ Θεοῦ (Matthew) in Z fam. 1 33 lat syˢᶜ and (Mark) syˢᶜ; *intrare per foramen* l.= (Matth. and Luk.) in syˢᶜ and (Mark) in syˢ.

We also may refer to Ephrem, *Comment. in Diat.* XV 1, where a *dives* asks: *Quid faciam ut vivam*, and answers: *Factum est a me hoc.* Aphraates reads: *Et diviti illi . . . et ait ei . . . Autem ei homo ille: Haec feci a iuventute mea . . . Vene, vende omnia quae habes.* Aphraates

---

[1] QUISPEL, *New Testament*, p. 191, HAENCHEN, *art. c.*, p. 164.
[2] VIELHAUER, *o.c.*, p. 96: Gospel of the Nazarenes.

omits καὶ ἕξεις . . . οὐρανοῖς and reads *Facilius est intrare camelum*.

It is striking that we find the reading *alter divitum*. One may suppose that another story about a rich man preceded. In T¹ and Tᵃ this pericope is really preceded by Luk. 12, 13-21 and followed by Luk. 16, 14-15 and 19-31. This means that we have three stories about riches one after the other [1]).

13. *Historia passionis Domini* f. 25 [2]: *Et sicut dicitur in evangelio Nazarenorum singulorum pedes osculatus fuit*. *Liber Graduum* XVI 4 shows an almost similar reading of John 13, 5[3].

14. Jerome, *de vir. ill.* 16, cf. *In Is.* XVIII *praef.* and Origen, *de princ.* I, *prooem.* 8: . . . *non sum daemonium incorporale*, see Luk. 24, 39. Also in Tᵖ and Titus of Bostra IV 37 [4].

15. Jerome, *Comment. in Matth.* 27, 16 [5]: βαρραββᾶν l. βαραββᾶν cum 69 g² syʰᵐᵍ.

16. Jerome, *Comment. in Ez.* 18, 7 [6]: . . . *inter maxima ponitur crimina, qui fratris sui spiritum contristaverit*. *Liber Graduum* V 9, VII 1, XI 19, XXVII 6, shows the same reading [7].

From this list a few interesting conclusions can be drawn. First of all it appears that most parallels with Jewish-Christian Gospel-fragments are met with in one or more versions of the Diatessaron (4, 5, 8 and 11). This does not mean that the variant readings were not present in some tetraevangelium. In 7, for example, we have an interesting agreement with Marcion. This last case renders impossible the simple conclusion that Tatian used a Jewish-Christian Gospel. Tatian may have used a Gospel-text which was influenced by Jewish-Christian Gospels. But it is also possible that a particular text of the Gospels both influenced the Diatessaron and the Jewish-Christian Gospels. This possibility provides a very good explanation of those agreements where a number of manuscripts are involved (6, 9, 10 and probably 15). Three parallels can be found only in Ev. Th. and *Liber Graduum*. We do not exclude the possibility that a Jewish-Christian Gospel or extra-canonical

---

[1] See A. F. J. KLIJN, "The Question of the Rich Young Man in a Jewish-Christian Gospel", in: *NT* 8 1966, p. 149-155.

[2] VIELHAUER, *o.c.*, p. 99: Gospel of the Nazarenes.

[3] See QUISPEL, "The 'Gospel of Thomas' and the 'Gospel of the Hebrews' ", in: *NTS* 12 1965/66, p. 371-382.

[4] See also KLIJN, *Survey*, p. 103-105.

[5] VIELHAUER, *o.c.*, p. 97: Gospel of the Nazarenes.

[6] VIELHAUER, *o.c.*, p. 108: Gospel of the Hebrews.

[7] QUISPEL, *Hebrews*, p. 374.

Gospel-tradition had a direct influence on these writings (3, 13 and 16) [1].

---

[1] Whether Ev. Th. in its *logia* of the synoptic type was influenced by an extra-canonical source has been debated. The idea has been rejected by HAENCHEN, *art. c.*, p. 162-165, and IDEM, "Die Botschaft des Thomas-Evangeliums", in: *Theol. Bibliothek Töpelmann* 6, Berlin 1961, p. 10; R. M. GRANT-D. N. FREEDMAN, *The Secret Sayings of Jesus*, London and Glasgow 1960, p. 102; W. MICHAELIS, "Das Thomas-Evangelium", in: *Calwer Hefte* 34, Stuttgart 1960; H. K. McARTHUR, "The Dependence of the Gospel of Thomas on the Synoptics", in: *ET* 71 1959/60, p. 286-287; SCHIPPERS, *o.c.*, and *idem*, "Het Evangelie van Thomas, een onafhankelijke Traditie", in: *GTT* 61 1961, p. 46-54; J. MUNCK, "Bemerkungen zum Thomasevangelium", in: *Studia Theol.* 14 1960, p. 130-147, esp. p. 139-141. Hesitating are R. KASSER, *L'Évangile selon Thomas*, Neuchâtel 1961, p. 18: R. McL. WILSON, *Studies in the Gospel of Thomas*, London 1960, p. 144-148, and *idem*, "Thomas and the Synoptic Gospels", in: *ET* 72 1960/61, p. 36-39, and B. GÄRTNER, *The Theology of the Gospel according to Thomas*, New York 1961, p. 53-55 and 63-65. For a more positive point of view see W. C. VAN UNNIK mit Beiträgen von JOH. BAUER und W. TILL, *Evangelien aus dem Nilsand*, Frankfurt am Main 1960, p. 61 and 65-67 (Van Unnik) and 122 (Bauer); O. CULLMANN, "Das Thomasevangelium und die Frage nach dem Alter der in ihm enthaltenen Tradition", in: *TL* 85 1962, c. 321-334, esp. c. 333. Cullmann pointed to the fact that these *logia* represent "das älteste christliche Traditionsgut". This "traditionsgeschichtliche" and "formgeschichtliche" approach to the Ev. Th. has led some scholars to the conclusion that extra-canonical material has been used. We refer to H.-W. BARTSCH, "Das Thomas-Evangelium und die synoptischen Evangelien", in: *NTS* 6 1959/60, p. 249-261; C. H. HUNZINGER, "Außersynoptischer Traditionsgut im Thomas-Evangelium", in: *TL* 85 1960, c. 843-846, and IDEM, "Unbekannte Gleichnisse Jesu aus dem Thomas-Evangelium", in: *Judentum Christentum Kirche*, Festschrift für J. JEREMIAS, in: *Beih. ZNW* 26, Berlin 1964, p. 209-220; H. MONTEFIORE, "A Comparison of the Parables of the Gospel acc. to Thomas and the synoptic Gospels", in: *NTS* 7 1960/61, p. 220-248, see also H. MONTEFIORE and H. E. W. TURNER, "Thomas and the Evangelists", in: *Stud. in Bibl. Theol.* 35, London 1962, p. 40-78; J. JEREMIAS, *Die Gleichnisse Jesu*, Göttingen 1965[7], esp. p. 86-87 and p. 198. We do not think that these studies are always convincing, cf. A. F. J. KLIJN, "Das Thomasevangelium und das altsyrische Christentum", in: *VC* 15 1961, p. 146-159, esp. p. 152, n. 35. See for the problem of the *logia*-source also R. NORTH, "Chenoboskion and Q", in: *CBQ* 24 1962, p. 154-170. See for Liber Graduum and Macarius: A. BAKER, "The Significance of the New Testament Text of the Syriac Liber Graduum", in: *Studia Evangelica* V, in: *TU* 103 1968, p. 171-175, p. 175: "Finally there appears to be some non-canonical source or sources from which some unusual versions of the New Testament texts are derived; ,IDEM "The 'Gospel of Thomas' and the Syriac 'Liber Graduum' ", in: *NTS* 12 1965/66, p. 49-55; IDEM, "Pseudo-Macarius and the Gospel of Thomas", in: *VC* 18 1964, p. 215-225, and Q. QUISPEL, "The Syrian Thomas and the Syrian Macarius", in: *idem* 226-235. See also A. BAKER, "Syriac and the scriptural Quotations of Pseudo-Macarius", in: *JTS* n. S. 20 1969, p. 133-149; IDEM, "The Gospel of Thomas and the Diatessaron", in: *JTS* n. S. 16 1965, p. 449-454, and R. STAATS, "Die törichten Jungfrauen von Mt 25 in gnostischer und antignostischer Literatur", in:

Two cases call for our special consideration (2 and 12). Early christian witnesses show a wide acquaintance with the readings in 2. It is of course possible that both Tatian and Justin were separately influenced by a Jewish-Christian tradition. It seems, however, much simpler to suppose that certain very ancient traditions influenced the text of the canonical Gospels which were used by Tatian, Justin and the Jewish-Christian Gospels. Example 12 shows some very interesting agreements between a Jewish-Christian Gospel and traditions in Syria. Here also the possibility of a particular text of the Gospel having influenced the Jewish-Christian Gospel and the Diatessaron cannot be excluded. But in this case we see that both the Jewish-Christian Gospel and the Diatessaron may bear witness to the same order of pericopes. This can hardly have been brought about accidentally. Here we cannot avoid the presumption that extra-canonical influence is the cause of Tatian's order of pericopes [1].

From this it appears how difficult it is to prove extra-canonical influence on the text of the Gospels. Even agreement with the fragment of the Jewish-Christian Gospels does not prove this influence. The reason for this conclusion is that we do not know very much of the canonical text of the Gospels in the area where we notice the agreement and that we must not forget that the Jewish-Christian Gospels made use of one or more of the canonical Gospels themselves.

But even if this last difficulty is absent, we cannot draw final conclusions. This is shown by the quotations in Ignatius. Smit Sibinga gives a few examples of passages where Ignatius obviously draws from an extra-canonical source. This was probably the source that Matthew used in composing his Gospel. We cite the following examples [2]:

Ignatius, *Rom.* VI 1: αἱ βασιλεῖαι τοῦ αἰῶνος τούτου 1.
Matthew 6, 8 τὰς βασιλείας τοῦ κόσμου cum sy[s]: ܟܠܗ ܡܠܟܘܬܐ ܕܥܠܡܐ.

W. ELTESTER, "Christentum und Gnosis", in: *Beiheft ZNW* of 1969, p. 98-115, p. 106, n. 17.

[1] See also the cumbrous way to show an extra-canonical reading in the Diatessaron-text of Luke 7, 43 in W. HENSS, "Das Verhältnis zwischen Diatessaron, christlicher Gnosis und 'Western Text' ", in: *Beih. ZNW* 33 1967, and *Review* by G. QUISPEL in: *NTT* 22 1967/68, p. 139-140.

[2] See J. SMIT SIBINGA, "Ignatius and Matthew", in: *NT* 8 1966, p. 263-283. Cf. also J. PAIRMAN BROWN, "The Form of 'Q' known to Matthew", in: *NTS* 8 1961/62, p. 27-42.

Smyrn. X I: οὐ μὴ ἀπολεῖται l.

Matthew 10. 42 οὐ μὴ ἀπολέσῃ cum D it sy[sc] bo

Eph. XVIII I: ἐπὶ τῆς κεφαλῆς l.

Mark 14, 3 αὐτοῦ τῆς κεφαλῆς in א B or κατὰ τῆς κεφαλῆς in A etc., cum D lat. sy[sp] sa bo, but cf. Matth. 26, 7.

Smyrn. VI I: ὁ χωρῶν χωρείτω, cf.

Matthew 19, 12 ὁ δυνάμενος χωρεῖν χωρείτω and

Mark 4, 9 ἔχει ὦτα ἀκούειν ἀκουέτω, but D it sy[hmg] add. ὁ συνίων συνιέτω.

We do not think that these cases are very convincing and we might even suppose that some of the examples are purely accidental. But even if the Western witnesses show agreement with a pre-Matthean text it remains an open question whether these Western witnesses give the original text which was altered in the other manuscripts or whether the Western witnesses were influenced by the pre-Matthean text.

We mentioned our lack of knowledge with regard to the canonical text in the Syriac area. To get some idea of this text we point to two writings: The *Epistula Apostolorum* and the Gospel of Peter. In both cases we are dealing with a pre-Tatianic text and in both cases we have a text which made use of the canonical Gospels. But in both writings we find the most striking agreement with the text of the Diatessaron and the Old Syriac. For the *Epistula Apostolorum* [1] we may refer to:

3 (14) lust des Fleisches l. θελήματος σαρκὸς (John 1, 13) cum T[1]

5 (16) lud ihn ein cf. *invitatus* l. *vocatus* (John 2, 2) cum b r[1], see also vs 1 add. *mater . . . invitata* in a ff[2] Ir

5 (16) Menschengedränge l. ὄχλον (Mark 5, 31) and οἱ ὄχλοι (Luk. 8, 45), but "the crowds of the people" in T[1] and *turbae hominum* in Ephrem [2].

We do not repeat the numerous examples of agreement with the Gospel of Peter and the Old Syriac text given by the present writer [3]. All of them show that before 150 in Syria a text existed which in many cases showed agreement with Tatian's Diatessaron.

---

[1] See M. HORNSCHUH, "Studien zur Epistula Apostolorum", in: *Patrist. Texte und Studien* 5, Berlin 1965, and H. DUENSING, "Epistula Apostolorum", in: *Kleine Texte* 152, Berlin 1925, p. 6-7.

[2] See PLOOY, *Liège Diatessaron*, p. 133.

[3] A. F. J. KLIJN, "Het Evangelie van Petrus en de Westerse Tekst", in: *NTT* 15 1960/61, p. 264-269.

We can be sure that this was the same text used by the composers of the so-called Jewish-Christian Gospels. This text deviated widely from the text which we—for the sake of convenience—call the "neutral text". The reason may be that the text in Syria —and we think in particular of the text in Antioch—grew up in an environment with a lively Gospel tradition. We may suppose a mutual influence of written and oral Gospel traditions. Particularly we may suppose a continuous effort to harmonise and to bring together these traditions, a procedure we know of from our canonical Matthew and Luke. As far as we can speak with confidence of the fragments of the Jewish-Christian Gospels we again and again find harmonisations. The same applies to quotations in the Apostolic Fathers, the Gospel of Thomas and the Diatessaron. It is not the variant readings but these harmonisations and the conflating of verses which strikes us [1]. If we, therefore, give our opinion with regard to the Jewish-Christian Gospels, the Gospel of Thomas and the Diatessaron, we consider all these writings as products of the way in which the Gospel tradition was handled. Because of the way this was done they were bound to bring together what we call canonical matter, viz. our canonical Gospels, and extra-canonical tradition. For this reason we believe that the place of origin of most of the readings in the Western text was a place where Gospel tradition was not limited to written Gospels, but where written and oral tradition had the same rights [2].

---

[1] A fine example of early harmonisation we find in Did. 1, 4-5 with parallels in Matth. 5, 39 (cf. Luk. 6, 29a); Matth. 5, 41; Luk. 6, 29b (cf. Matth. 5, 40); Luk. 6, 30 (cf. Matth. 5, 42), see H. Köster, "Synoptische Überlieferung bei den apostolischen Vätern", in: *TU* 65 1957, p. 227-228. Aphraates IX 6 (Matth. 5, 39; Matth. 5, 41; Luk. 6, 29b) and Liber Graduum II 2 (Matth. 5, 39; Matth. 5, 41; Luk. 6, 29b) are in striking agreement with the Didache. It is not acceptable that the Diatessaron depends on the Didache (cf. G. Dix, "Didache and Diatessaron", in: *JTS* 34 1933, p. 242-250, and R. H. Connolly, "Didache and Diatessaron", in: *idem*, p. 346-347). We suppose that an ancient extra-canonical Gospel tradition influenced both the Didache and the early Syriac authors. In this case we also assume that the extra-canonical material is also pre-canonical, see B. Layton, "The Sources and Transmission of *Didache* 1.3b-2.1", in: *HTR* 61 1968, p. 343-383.

[2] We do not believe that Edessa was a centre of text-corruption. We rather suppose that it was Antioch. Maybe, corruption found its way from this town to Edessa. We reject the adventurous ideas which appear to be popular to-day that Edessa received the Gospel and the Gospel-tradition from Jerusalem, cf. J. C. L. Gibson, "From Qumran to Edessa or the Aramaic-Speaking Church before and after 70 A.D." in: *The Annual of the Leeds Univ. Oriental Society* V 1963-1965; H. Köster, "ΓΝΩΜΑΙ ΔΙΑΦΟ-

With regard to the Diatessaron some work has been done in the field of the Latin offshoot of this work. Quispel notices some agreement between the Diatessaron and the old Saxon poem called the Heliand. This relation had already been noticed a long time ago, but usually one did not go further than pointing to the agreement with the vulgatized Fuldensis and Amiatinus. Now Quispel has drawn some instances into the picture where the Heliand is in agreement with Ev. Th. Not all these instances were acceptable to the Germanist W. Krogmann who doubted whether Quispel was dealing with real variant readings. He explained them from a purely linguistic point of view [1].

For this reason it is to be welcomed that a Germanist J. J. van Weringh has taken up the matter [2]. He deals with 57 variant readings in the Heliand deviating from the Vulgate. "Most of the readings discussed . . . have been selected from a collection brought together at the Theological Seminar of Utrecht State University under the direction of Prof. Dr. G. Quispel . . ." [3]. At the end of this study the author gives a list in which we can see the support of the different Greek, Latin and Syriac texts of the New Testament and the Diatessaron as represented by the versions in the West and in the East [4]. From this list it appears that 21 readings are supported by the Dutch Diatessara only, three readings are supported by the Eastern Diatessara only. This means that 28 variant readings are supported by versions of the Diatessaron in both the West and the East. From these we can withdraw two readings because they are supported by sy^p. Thus the result is that 26 readings can be considered to be in agreement with the Diatessaron. Van Weringh is justified in saying that the Heliand seems to have used

---

POI. The Origin and Nature of Diversification in the History of the Early Christianity", in: *HTR* 58 1965, p. 279-318; G. QUISPEL, "The Discussion of Judaic Christianity", in: *VC* 22 1968, p. 81-93; L. W. BARNARD, "The Origin and Emergence of the Church in Edessa during the First two Centuries A.D.", in: *VC* 22 1968, p. 151-175.

[1] G. QUISPEL, "Some Remarks on the Gospel of Thomas", in: *NTS* 5 1959, p. 276-290; W. KROGMANN, "Heliand, Tatian und Thomasevangelium", in: *ZNW* 51 1960, p. 255-268; G. QUISPEL, "Der Heiland und das Thomasevangelium in: *VC* 16 1962, p. 121-153, and W. KROGMANN, "Heliand und Thomasevangelium", in: *VC* 18 1964, p. 65-73.

[2] J. J. VAN WERINGH, *Heliand and Diatessaron*, Assen 1965, also as Dr. JUW FON WERINGHA, "Heliand and Diatessaron", in: *Studia Germanica* V, Assen 1965.

[3] VAN WERINGH, *o.c.*, p. 46, n. 226.

[4] VAN WERINGH, *o.c.*, p. 133-134.

a text which is related with the Dutch versions of the Diatessaron.

With regard to this study we must remark that not less than 29 from the 57 readings come from Matth. 1 and Luke 1 and 2. We do not know what this means, but Pickering has said that the Heliand probably used Pseudo-Matthew [1]. If this is true, the influence of the Diatessaron did not come about directly, but by way of a popular account of Jesus' birth.

We do not think that this study gives us new views on the development of the Diatessaron. It was already known and it has been shown again that the Dutch version of the Diatessaron is related to the Diatessaron composed by Tatian and that the Dutch Diatessaron was popular in certain circles in the Church in the Low Countries.

b) THE SYRIAC TRANSLATIONS

Until about 20 years ago F. C. Burkitt's conclusions with regard to the development of the Syriac text were almost generally accepted. The opinion was that Tatian composed his Diatessaron about 170, that about 200, maybe due to Palut, the four separated Gospels were introduced and that finally about 411 Rabbula made a recension of the Syriac text known as the Peshitto. That something must be wrong in this hypothesis was shown by M. Black who pointed to a Peshitto manuscript with many Old Syriac readings and to the quotations in Jacob of Serug († 521) who uses a text akin to the Old Syriac version. But Black still believed that Rabbula had something to do with the birth of the Peshitto [2].

This last idea has been rejected by Vööbus on numerous occasions. He has shown that "Peshitto-readings" are discernable in the Old Syria text and that "Old Syriac-readings" are found long after Rabbula [3].

---

[1] F. P. PICKERING, "Christlicher Erzählstoff bei Otfrid und im Heliand", in: *Zeitschr. f. Deutsches Altertum und Deutsche Literatur* 85 1954, p. 262-291.

[2] M. BLACK, "Rabbula and the Peshitta", in: *BJRL* 33 1950, p. 203-210; IDEM, "The Text of the Peshitta Tetraevangelium", in: *Studia Paulina* in hon. J. DE ZWAAN, Haarlem 1953, p. 20-27, and IDEM, "The Gospel Text of Jacob of Serug", in: *JTS* n. S. 2 1951, p. 57-63.

[3] A. VÖÖBUS, "Investigations into the Text of the New Testament used by Rabbula of Edessa", in: *Contrib. of Baltic Univ.* 59, Pinneberg 1947; IDEM, "Researches on the Circulation of the Peshitta in the Middle of the Fifth Century", in: *idem* 64 1948; IDEM, "Neue Ergebnisse in der Erforschung der Geschichte der Evangelientexte im Syrischen", in: *idem* 65 1948; IDEM, "The oldest extant Traces of the Syriac Peshitta", in: *Le Muséon* 63 1950,

This means that the text in Syria shows a gradual growth. Vööbus' work has been generally accepted [1]. But some details are still waiting for clarification. For example, in the Life of Rabbula we read that Rabbula "translated by the wisdom of God that was in him the New Testament from Greek into Syriac, because of its variations, exactly as it was". It was Baarda who tried to shed light on this statement, by investigating the quotations in the "Life". Careful reading yielded a number of quotations and allusions from which conclusions can be drawn. The result is interesting. To some extent Vööbus' views are corroborated. In many cases the text is in agreement with the Diatessaron and the Western texts against sy[scp]. This means that the "Life" shows a very ancient text with readings which have been obviously revised in the well known Syriac manuscripts.

But this conclusion does not hold for John. In quotations from this Gospel the text shows some relation with sy[p]. From this Baarda draws the conclusion that Rabbula made "a more accurate translation of the passages that were important in the christological discussion among the Edessenian clergy" [2].

---

p. 191-204, about Peshitta-readings in Ps. Clement., *Recognitiones*. The results were criticized by M. BLACK, "Zur Geschichte des syrischen Evangelientextes", in: *TL* 77 1952, c. 705-710; A. VÖÖBUS, "Studies in the History of the Gospel Text in Syria", in: *GSCO* 128, Subsidia 3, Louvain 1951; IDEM, "A Critical Apparatus for the Vetus Syra", in: *JBL* 70 1951, p. 123-128; IDEM, "Neuentdecktes Textmaterial zur Vetus Syra", in: *TZ* 7 1951, p. 30-38; IDEM, "Neue Angaben über die textgeschichtlichen Zustände: in Edessa in den Jahren ca 326-340", in: *Papers of the Estonian Theol. Soc. in Exile* 2/1951; IDEM, "Die Evangelienzitate in der Einleitung der Persischen Märtyrerakten", in: *Bibl* 33 1952, p. 222-234; IDEM, "Neue Materialen zur Geschichte der Vetus Syra in den Evangelienhandschriften", in: *Papers of the Estonian Theol. Soc. in Exile* 5, Stockholm 1953; IDEM, "Early Versions of the New Testament", in: *idem* 6 1954; IDEM "Das Alter der Peshitta", in: *OC* 38 1954; IDEM, "Completion of the Vetus Syra Project", in: *Biblical Research* 7 1962, p. 49-56.

[1] His remarks on the Diatessaron are rather superficial, cf. Vööbus, *Studies in the History . . .*, p. 17, about the Gospel of the Hebrews in Syria, and p. 18, about a fifth source used by Tatian. See also criticism of Vööbus' views with regard to Ephrem's supposed remarks on the Greek New Testament which really are interpolations: J. P. SMITH, *Review* of Vööbus *Studies*, in: *Bibl* 33 1z52, p. 545-549. See also *Review* his *Early Versions* by W. P. M. McHARDY, in: *JTS* n. S. 3 1952, p. 264-266; E. MASSAUX, in: *Le Muséon* 68 1955, p. 422-431, and H. ENGBERDING, in: *OC* 40 1956, p. 142-143, and of his *Neue Angaben* by B.-M. BOISMARD, in: *RB* 59 1954, p. 271-272.

[2] TJ. BAARDA, "The Gospel Text in the Biography of Rabbula", in: *VC* 14 1960, p. 102-127, p. 127.

This study is about the only one which appeared on the Old
Syriac translations since Vööbus' work [1].

c) Translations Dependent on the Syriac Version

In 1949 it was already known that the Armenian text shows some
relations with the Caesarean text and that in the quotations in
ecclesiastical authors a text is found more or less in agreement
with the Diatessaron. In a special study devoted to the Armenian
text Lyonnet concluded from these quotations that it can be
accepted that a Syriac text is the basis of the Armenian translation.
Lyonnet is incined to suppose a Syriac Diatessaron as underlying
this translation [2].

Vööbus doubted whether a Diatessaron was the first Armenian
text of the Gospels. He believed that the readings in agreement
with the Diatessaron in the Armenian version can be readily
explained from a Syriac tetraevangelium with many more Tatia-
nisms than are known in sy^s and sy^c [3].

Lyonnet showed that, as in Syria, an Old Armenian text was
only gradually replaced by the later Armenian Vulgate. It is
impossible to say in accordance with what kind of Greek manuscript
the different revisions took place. The Caesarean readings in the
Armenian version may be due to a Caesarean Greek manuscript,
but they may also be explained by the underlying Syriac text [4].

The Georgian version shows the same picture as the Armenian
version. An Old Georgian text (geo^1) with many readings agreeing
with the Old Armenian and the Old Syriac and showing Syriasms,
has been replaced, probably in the sixth or seventh century, by a

---

[1] See TJ. Baarda, "Dionysius Bar Salībī and the Text of Luk. I. 35",
in: VC 17 1963, p. 225-229; H. Quecke, "Lk 1, 34 in den alten Übersetzungen", in: Bibl 44 1963, p. 499-510, and Idem, "Lk 1, 34 im Diatessaron",
in: Bibl 45 1964, p. 85-88.

[2] S. Lyonnet, "Les Origines de la Version Arménienne et le Diatessaron",
in: BO 13 Roma 1950, cf. L. Mariès, Le Diatessaron à l'Origine de la Version
Arménienne", in: RSR 38 1951, p. 247-256. The same opinion in C. S. C.
Williams, Alterations to the Text of the Synoptic Gospels and Acts, Oxford
1951, and H. Vogels, in a Review of Lyonnet's Book in: TL 76 1951,
c. 544-545.

[3] Vööbus, Early Versions, p. 142, and Idem, "La Première Traduction
Arménienne des Évangiles", in: RSR 1950, p. 581-586.

[4] See Lyonnet, Les Origines, p. 275; Vööbus, Early Versions, p. 169-170.
As we are ignorant of the history of the Armenian text, it remains difficult
to evaluate newly discovered manuscripts, cf. A. F. J. Klijn, "An old
Witness of the Armenian Text", in: JTS 52 1951, p. 168-170.

text (geo²) which was obviously influenced by some Greek text [1].

Vööbus considers the Ethiopian text to be a mixed text in which we can discern traces of the Old Syriac, Greek, Coptic and Arabic. The Arabic version was, according to Vööbus, influenced by the Syriac and Coptic version [2].

It is clear that all these conclusions are only tentative. We are still used to speaking about *the* Armenian and *the* Ethiopian translation but our knowledge only rests upon a very limited number of manuscripts. Literally hundreds and hundreds of manuscripts of these secondary translations are waiting to be collated [3].

---

[1] Editions: R. P. BLAKE and M. BRIÈRE, "The Old Georgian Version of the Gospels with the Variants of the Opiza and Tbet' Gospels. Edited with a Latin Translation", in: *Patrol. Orient.* 26. 4, Paris 1950; J. MOLITOR, "Das Adysh-Tetraevangelium", in: *OC* 37 1953, p. 30-35; 38 1954, p. 11-40; 39 1955, p. 1-32; 40 1956, p. 1-15; 41 1957, p. 1-21; 42 1958, p. 1-18; 43 1959, p. 1-16; 44 1960, p. 1-16; 45 1961, p. 1-8; 46 1962, p. 1-18; 47 1963, p. 1-15. See also *idem*, "Chanmetifragmente. Ein Beitrag zur Textgeschichte der altgeorgischen Bibelübersetzung", in: *idem* 41 1957, p. 22-34; 43 1959, p. 17-23; 44 1960, p. 17-24; 45 1961, p. 115-126; 46 1962, p. 19-24. J. MOLITOR, "Die Bedeutung der altgeorgischen Bibel für die neutestamentliche Textkritik", in: *BZ* 4 1960, p. 39-53. See also G. GARITTE, "L'Ancienne Version Géorgienne des Actes des Apôtres", in: *Bibl. du Muséon* 38, Louvain 1955; J. MOLITOR, "Die Georgische Bibelübersetzung", in: *OC* 37 1953, p. 23-29; VÖÖBUS, *Early Versions*, p. 175, and A. VÖÖBUS, "Zur Geschichte des altgeorgischen Evangelientextes", in: *Papers of the Estonian Theol. Soc. in Exile* 4 1953. See also METZGER, *Text* (sec. ed.), p. 268.

[2] A. VÖÖBUS, "Die Spuren eines älteren Äthiopischen Evangelientextes im Lichte der literarischen Monumente", in: *Papers . . . in Exile* 2 1951, and *idem, Early Versions*, p. 263-265 and p. 294-285.

[3] See E. F. RHODES, "An Annotated List of Armenian New Testament Manuscripts", in: *Annual Report of Theology*, Monograph Series vol. I, Ikebukuro, Tokyo, Japan 1959, see addition by A. WIKGREN, in: *JBL* 79 1960, p. 52-56.

CHAPTER TWO

EGYPT

Westcott and Hort knew only one text in Egypt: the Alexandrian Text. Witnesses to this text were, for example, the manuscripts C and L and authors like Origen. This Alexandrian text was supposed to be a recension of the "Neutral Text", which was not a local text but the original text, represented by the manuscripts א and B. The Alexandrian text was, according to Westcott and Hort, a good text in comparison with the Western Text and the Syrian Text, because in Egypt the "Neutral Text" happened to be the oldest text.

This supposition had already been challenged by the end of last century when Barnard proved that Clement of Alexandria used a Western Text [1]. This raised the question whether the "Neutral Text" really could be said to be the oldest text in Egypt. How this question was answered can be seen in the books of two leading textual critics in the first quarter of this century.

Lake showed that the existence of a Western Text was not only proved by the quotations in Clement but also by the text of the Sahidic version. For this reason he came to the conclusion that Westcott and Hort underestimated the great antiquity of the Western Text. According to Lake evidence shows that the Western Text "existed in the earliest times of which we have any certain knowledge—both in Syriac, Latin, and Greek speaking circles; in the East, in Africa, in Italy, and in Gaul". To these regions he added Egypt. He stated that "the Neutral text in

---

[1] P. M. BARNARD, "The Biblical Text of Clement of Alexandria", in: *T and S* V 1899, see also R. J. SWANSON, *The Gospel Text of Clement of Alexandria*, Ph. D. Diss. Yale University 1956, drawing the conclusion that Clement used a text like א for Matthew and John and like D in Luke (p. 173). "The evidence presented in our investigation indicates that the Egyptian and Western Texts were current in Alexandria at the end of the second century". Not available were: M. MEES, *Die Zitate aus dem Neuen Testament bei Klemens von Alexandrien*, Dissert. Pontif. Instit. Biblic., Roma 1966, and IDEM, "Papyrus Bodmer XIV (P⁷⁵) und die Lukaszitate bei Clemens von Alexandrien", in: *Studi e Ricerche di Scienze Religione in onore dei Santi Apostoli Pietro e Paolo nel XIX centenario del loro martirio*, Roma. Facultas Theologica Pontificae Universitatis Lateranensis 1967, p. 97-120.

Alexandria began at some date between Clement and Origen". And his final conclusion was that "the B text is merely an early form of the Alexandrian text" [1].

Lake thus relegated the אB text to the rank of one of the local texts in the early centuries of the Church. With this opinion the basis of Westcott and Hort's history of the text is completely undermined.

Streeter, the other famous textual critic, had to evaluate the same data. He also pointed to the Western readings in Clement and the Sahidic version. He does not deny that Western readings existed in Egypt. He even has an eye for these readings in the manuscript א, L, C and 33. He goes so far as to say that actually not one "Alexandrian Manuscript" has escaped the influence of the Western Text. But, unlike Lake, he supposed that this text entered Egypt during a second stage after a time during which a א B text alone was used. According to Streeter, the Western Text might have been introduced by Roman christians. It is true that Clement, the oldest known author in Egypt, used a Western text, but this can be explained by his sojourn in South Italy [2].

We may say that in 1930 these two opinions existed:

1. The Alexandrian Text with אB is secondary and is the result of the revision of a text akin to what is known as the Western Text (Lake).

2. The Alexandrian Text goes back to a text which is best preserved in B. It is a genuine Egyptian text which was influenced by Western readings at a later stage (Streeter).

A few years later P[45] was discovered. The manuscript had to be evaluated in the light of the existing types of text. But Kenyon who published the papyrus with an introduction, admitted that the manuscript did not show any decisive preference for one of the well known types of text, the Neutral, the Alexandrian, the Western or the Byzantine [3]. This conclusion could have led to the question whether the classical division of manuscripts is in accordance with the true history of the text. For here was a manuscript which did not fit into anyone of these types. This possibility, however, was immediately not thought of.

---

[1] K. LAKE, The Text of the New Testament, London 1904[3], p. 78 and 70.
[2] B. H. STREETER, The Four Gospels, London 1926, p. 56-57.
[3] F. C. KENYON, The Chester Beatty Biblical Papyri ..., Fasc. II: The Gospels and Acts. Text, London 1938, p. XIV.

The reason for this steady adherence to the well known grouping
of texts was probably the discovery of a new type of text, the
Caesarean Text, to which P[45] seemed to belong. Kenyon wrote:
"it is clear that the papyrus has a strong affinity with the group
which has of late years been identified ... with the text of
Caesarea" [1].

P[45] had been added to an existing type of text. The discovery
of the papyrus did not make it necessary to change anything in
the generally accepted division of the manuscripts into five groups.
Because P[45] has been assigned to the text of Caesarea, it was no
longer even necessary to take it seriously with regard to the history
of the text in Egypt!

This last statement held good as long as one believed that the
Caesarean Text was the result of a revision which took place in
Caesarea. But investigations into the text have shown that the
text has to be divided into two groups: a pre-Caesarean Text
consisting of P[45] [2] W fam. 1 28 and fam. 13 and the Caesarean
Text proper consisting of Θ 565 700 Origen, Eusebius sy[s] the Old
Georgian and the Old Armenian [3]. The pre-Caesarean Text was
supposed to have had its origin in Egypt [4].

This division posed the question how P[45] and the other members
of the pre-Caesarean Text had to be fitted into the history of the
text in Egypt. The question could have been satisfactorily answered
if we had only known something about the origin of the pre-Caesarean Text. We can only say something about the origin, if we know
something about the character of a text. And here we hit on the
real difficulty of this text: nobody can describe what kind of text
the Caesarean really represents. The general opinion can best
be given by quoting some words written by Metzger: "The special

---

[1] KENYON, o.c., p. XV.

[2] Cf. H. W. HUSTON, "Mark 6 and 11 in P[45] and the Caesarean Text",
in: *JBL* 74 1955, p. 262-271.

[3] See KLIJN, *Survey*, p. 110-117; B. M. METZGER, "The Caesarean Text of
the Gospels", in: *Chapters in the History of New Testament Textual Criticism*,
in: *NTTS* IV 1963, p. 42-72, p. 64, and E. F. HILLS, "The Inter-Relationship
of the Caesarean Manuscripts", in: *JBL* 68 1949, p. 141-159. See for pre-
Caesarean readings in Photius: J. N. BIRDSALL, "The Text of the Gospels
in Photius", in: *JTS* n. S. 7 1956, p. 42-55 and 190-198 and IDEM, "Photius
and the Text of the Fourth Gospel", in: *NTS* 4 1957/58, p. 61-63.

[4] See METZGER, *Caesarean Text*, p. 63, and *idem*, *Text*, p. 215: "The Old
Egyptian text which Origen brought with him to Caesarea may be called
the pre-Caesarean text".

character of the Caesarean text is its distinctive mixture of Western readings and Alexandrian readings" [1]. It appears that the number of readings in the Caesarean Text which can not be found in any of the other types of text is very small.

This phenomenon immediately raises the question whether this Caesarean Text should not be explained by the influence of an Alexandrian Text on a Western Text or a Western Text on an Alexandrian Text. This alternative view starts from the supposition that these two texts existed at an early date. It is also possible to suppose that originally a text existed with readings now discernable in different types of text. In that case we are not dealing with a "mixed text" but with a pre-recensional text or a "wild" text with all the readings still present in one text which have been distributed over a number of texts at a later stage.

These possibilities remind us of the difference between Lake and Streeter. In general scholars seemed to be inclined to suppose a pre-recensional text at the basis of the Alexandrian [2].

Since 1949 the investigation into the Caesarean Text has been directed to the quotations from early Egyptian and Palestinian authors.

The results are interesting because the quotations in Origen [3] and Eusebius [4] show the same picture as the text of an early papyrus like P[45]. Side by side we find quotations agreeing with Alexandrian, Caesarean and Western manuscripts. Generally speaking the quotations in Origen show a tendency to support the Alexandrian Text and in Eusebius the Western Text. Nowhere,

---

[1] METZGER, *Text*, p. 215.

[2] There had been written only very few articles on the text of Egypt, cf. H. A. SANDERS, "The Egyptian Text of the Four Gospels and Acts", in: *HTR* 26 1933, p. 177-198, and P. L. HEDLEY, "The Egyptian Text of the Gospels and Acts", in: *Church Quarterly Rev.* 118 1934, p. 33-39 and 188-230.

[3] K. W. KIM, "The Matthean Text of Origen in his commentary on Matthew", in: *JBL* 68 1949, p. 125-139; IDEM, "Origen's Text of Matthew in his Against Celsus", in: *JTS* n. S. 4 1953, p. 42-49, and IDEM, "Origen's Text of John in his On Prayer, Commentary on Matthew and Against Celsus", in: *JTS* n. S. 7 1956, p. 74-84.

[4] See H. S. MURPHEY, "Eusebius' New Testament Text in the Demonstratio Evangelica", in: *JBL* 73 1954, p. 162-168; M. J. SUGGS, "Eusebius' Text of John in the 'Writings against Marcellus' ", in: *JBL* 75 1956, p. 137-142; IDEM, "The Eusebian Text of Matthew" in: *NT* 1 1956, p. 233-245; D. VOLTURNO, *Four Gospel Text of Eusebius*, Ph. D., Boston University 1956, and D. S. WALLACE-HADRILL. "Eusebius and the Gospel Text of Caesarea", in: *HTR* 49 1956, p. 105-114.

however, do we see these authors consistently following one of the well known types of text. A change occurs, however, when we check the quotations in Athanasius [1], Didymus the Blind [2] and Cyril of Jerusalem [3]. Here we meet agreement with the Alexandrian type of text.

The results of all this can be found in the text-books, where the manuscripts from Egypt and the quotations in Egyptian authors are usually divided into four groups: the Western (Clement), the Alexandrian (א B C L etc.), the Caesarean (P[45]) and the Byzantine (later manuscripts) [4]. This division is not satisfactory because it is based on a similarity of readings only. We do not wish to maintain that this similarity is often of only the remotest character, but we must state that this division does not answer vital questions about the chronological or material relationship between these types of text. This means that this grouping does not tell us anything about the most important question of the history of the text in Egypt.

Thus the investigation into the text of Egypt threatened to end

---

[1] G. ZERVOPOULOS, *The Gospel-Text of Athanasius*, Ph. D. Boston University 1955.

[2] W. C. LINSS, *The Four Gospel Text of Didymus the Blind*, D. Theol. Boston Univ. 1955.

[3] J. H. GREENLEE, "The Gospel Text of Cyril of Jerusalem", in: *S and D* XVII Copenhagen 1955, reviewed by R. V. G. TASKER, in: *JTS* n. S. 7 1956, p. 278-288.

[4] See METZGER, *Text*, p. 214-216, and J. H. GREENLEE, *Introduction*, p. 117. The only one who has tried to offer a fresh division of the manuscripts is M.-E. Boismard. One of the main characteristics of the oldest text and the quotations in the earliest ecclesiastical writers is, according to Boismard, its shortness, see M.-E. BOISMARD, "A Propos de Jean V, 39. Essai de Critique Textuelle", in: *RB* 55 1948, p. 5-34; IDEM, "Critique Textuelle et Citations Patristiques", in: *idem* 57 1950, p. 381-408; IDEM, "Lectio Brevior Potior", in: *idem* 58 1951, p. 161-168, and IDEM, "Problèmes de Critique Textuelle concernant le quatrième Évangile", in: *idem* 60 153, p. 347 371. This short Text can be found in Tatian, the Old Latin and the Old Syriac version, the Georgian, Persian and Ethiopian version. Apart from this group Boismard supposes a group called *B* represented by B, Origen, C W L 33 sa and bo and א partially. Next he points to a group called *SD* which is to be found in D and א partially. Finally we have a group called *C*, the Caesarean Text. Boismard has distributed the Western witnesses over two groups: the old versional text and the אD-text. The relation between א and D is evident, cf. B. BOTTE, "Un Témoin du Texte Césaréen de quatrième Évangile: l 253", in: *Mél. Bibl. A. Robert* Travaux de l'Institut Cath. de Paris 4 1956, p. 466-469. We doubt, however, whether any grouping of manuscripts gives satisfactory results.

in a dead-lock, until the question was reopened by the discovery of two new papyri:

P⁶⁶ (Bodmer II). This papyrus of the Gospel of John was edited in two parts. In 1956 V. Martin published chapters 1 to 14 ¹ and in 1958 chapters 14-21 ². In 1962 followed a "Nouvelle Édition augmentée et corrigée" with a photographic reproduction by V. Martin and J. W. B. Barns ³. In a number of articles corrections have been added to these publications by Barns ⁴, Boismard and Roux ⁵ and Aland ⁶. The manuscript has been dated about 200 ⁷.

P⁷⁵ (Bodmer XIV-XV). This papyrus of the Gospel of John chapters 1 to 15 and Luke chapters 3 to 24, has been edited by V. Martin and R. Kasser ⁸. The manuscript has been assigned to the third century.

The outward appearance of the two manuscripts is quite different. P⁶⁶ was written by a scribe who tried to produce a faithful text. He does not hesitate to correct his errors, both during his copying of the text, and also after finishing the manuscript. This second correction may have been done by an other person who apparently made use of a manuscript different from the copy from which the scribe originally took the text.

The scribe of P⁷⁵ was careful and accurate. He copied his text

---

¹ Papyrus Bodmer II. *Évangile de Jean chap. 1-14*. Publié par Victor Martin. Bibliotheca Bodmeriana 1956.

² Papyrus Bodmer II, *Supplément. Évangile de Jean chap. 14-21*. Publié par Victor Martin. Bibliotheca Bodmeriana 1958.

³ Papyrus Bodmer II. *Supplément. Évangile de Jean chap. 14-21*. Publié par Victor Martin et J. W. B. Barns. *Nouvelle Édition augmentée et corrigée avec reproduction photographique complète du manuscrit (chap. 1-21)*. Bibliotheca Bodmeriana 1962.

⁴ J. W. B. Barns, "Papyrus Bodmer II. Some Corrections and Remarks", in: *Le Muséon* 75 1962, p. 327-329.

⁵ M.-E. Boismard, "Papyrus Bodmer II. Supplément de Jean . . . 1962", in: *RB* 70 1962, p. 120-133.

⁶ K. Aland, "Neue Neutestamentliche Papyri II", in: *NTS* 10 1963/64 1 p. 62-79.

⁷ H. Hunger, "Zur Datierung des Papyrus Bodmer II (P⁶⁶) (mit 1 Tafel)", in: *Anzeiger der phil.-hist. Kl. der Österreichischen Akademie der Wissensch.* 1960, nr. 4, p. 12-23, and K. Aland, "Neue Neutestamentliche Papyri II", in: *NTS* 9 1962, p. 302-316, p. 308.

⁸ Papyrus Bodmer XIV. *Évangile de Luc chap. 3-24*. Publié par Victor Martin et Rudolphe Kasser. Bibliotheca Bodmeriana 1961, and Papyrus Bodmer XV. *Évangile de Jean chap. 1-15*. Publié par Victor Martin et Rudolphe Kasser. Bibliotheca Bodmerina 1961. See K. Aland, "Neue Neutestamentliche Papyri II", in: *NTS* 11 1964/65, p. 1-21.

faithfully without correcting his errors, indeed without needing to correct errors [1].

Again textual critics had to fit these manuscripts into the existing groups. This could only be done by comparing these papyri with other manuscripts. The greatest resulting surprise was that P75 appeared to show a text which is in very close agreement with B. This means that we can say with Martini who studied the relation between B and P75 that the archetype of P75 and B must go back to a time "non più tardi della fine del seculo II" [2].

This conclusion can not be doubted. In addition to this it agrees with what we know of the text of the oldest extant scrap of Papyrus, P52, which also has a "Neutral Text". The two papyri demonstrate that in the middle of the second century, may be even earlier, a text like B was in use in Egypt.

This conclusion means that we can no longer maintain that this text was the result of a recension produced in the third century [3]. It is also impossible to say that this text originated after Clement of Alexandria, just because he used a Western Text. Now it is certain that even before Clement a text like B was in use.

The character of P66 is much more difficult to define than that of P75. Aland noticed a relation with P45 [4]. This does not mean that P45 and P66 have much in common. It only means that in the two manuscripts we find the same "mixture" of readings coming from different types of text. Birdsall has shown that P66 can not be fitted into the classical division of text. He supposes that P66 belongs to an area in which such types were not yet clearly distinguishable.

Birdsall is quite right, but we can only evaluate a manuscript by comparing it with other manuscripts or types of text. Birdsall himself can not avoid saying: "We might utilize some such terms as 'proto-Caesarean' for P45 and 'proto-Alexandrian' for P66". To this statement he adds that this "does not explain in any wise how the papyrus texts come to be what they are, but indicates that

---

[1] See E. C. COLWELL, "Scribal Habits in early Papyri. A Study in the Corruption of the Text", in: *The Bible in Modern Scholarship*, ed. by J. PH. HYATT, Nashville-New York 1965, p. 370-389, p. 381-382.

[2] C. M. MARTINI, "Il problema delle recensonalità de Codice B alle luce de papiro Bodmer XIV", in: *Analecta Biblica* 26, Roma 1966.

[3] See K. ALAND, "The Significance of the Papyri for Progress in New Testament Research", in: *The Bible ... Scholarship*, p. 325-346, 338.

[4] K. ALAND, "Neue Neutestamentliche Papyri II", in: *NTS* 9 1962 63, p. 302-316. See also J. N. BIRDSALL, *The Bodmer Papyri of the Gospel of John*, London 1960, p. 9.

the later text have, by some process of recension not yet traced in detail, been derived from the textual material which we sample here or in citations such as for example made by Clement of Alexandria" [1]. This is rather vague but we get the impression that Birdsall wants to say that the "mixed" or "wild" texts like P[45] and P[66] were the basis upon which by way of a recensional choice the Alexandrian Text was composed. Here we are back with Lake's opinion we referred to above.

Boismard's conclusions differ from those of Birdsall. He argues that P[66] bears witness to two types of text existing in Egypt. These types are called *B* and *SD*. Type *B* has a representative in the manuscript B. Type *SD* is a Western Text which has not been influenced by the Diatessaron. According to Boismard we find in P[66] readings of both types [2].

We may say that research has been dominated by the controversy we meet with in Birdsall and Boismard. For example, Collwell draws a conclusion similar to that of Birdsall when he says that "The 'Beta texttype' " must be considered a " 'made' text . . . produced in part by the selection of relatively 'good old MSS' but more importantly by the philological and editorial know-how of Alexandrians" [3]. Against this opinion we find H. Zimmermann drawing the following conclusion: "Man hat damit zu rechnen, dass der sog. Westliche Text schon in so früher Zeit (sc. 200) in Ägypten vorhanden ist und in den dort verbreiteten 'neutralen' Text eindrängt" [4]. Klijn also argued that a Western Text existed in Egypt alongside a B-text [5].

---

[1] See BIRDSALL, *o.c.*, p. 10.

[2] M.-E. BOISMARD, "Le Papyrus Bodmer II", in: *RB* 64 1957, p. 362-398. See for groups created by BOISMARD p. 36, n. 4

[3] E. C. COLWELL, "The Origin of Texttypes of New Testament Manuscripts", in: *Mélanges Willoughby*, ed. A. WIKGREN, Chicago 1961, p. 128-138, p. 137; cf. also C. L. PORTER, "An Analysis of the Textual Variation between Pap[75] and Codex Vaticanus in the Text of John", in: *Studies in the History and Text of the New Testament in honor of* K. W. CLARK by B. L. DANIELS and M. J. SUGGS, in: *S and D* XXIX 1967, p. 71-80; IDEM, "Papyrus Bodmer XV (P[75]) and the Text of Codex Vaticanus", in: *JBL* 81 1962, p. 363-376; B. M. METZGER, "The Bodmer Papyrus of Luke and John", in: *ET* 73 1961/62, p. 201-203, and K. W. CLARK, "The Text of the Gospel of John in third-century Egypt", in: *NT* 5 1962, p. 17-24.

[4] H. ZIMMERMANN, "Papyrus Bodmer II und seine Bedeutung für die Textgeschichte des Johannes-Evangeliums", in: *BZ* n.F. 2 1958, p. 214-243, p. 223.

[5] A. F. J. KLIJN, "Papyrus Bodmer II (John I-XIV) and the Text of Egypt", in: *NTS* 3 1956/67, p. 327-334.

Finally we refer to the conclusions of Kieffer. They are based
upon a study of the variant readings in John 6, 52-71. According
to him P⁶⁶ represents a "texte sauvage" and B is the product of a
"recension". This is roughly the opinion of Birdsall. Kieffer,
however, cannot deny that P⁶⁶ has already been influenced by a
recensional text and says: "il semble utiliser concoitement un ms
'sauvage' et un ms recensé" [1]. But this means that the recensional
text must go back to a date in the middle of the second century.

With this last variation the opinions are quite clear: some
consider P⁷⁵-B to be a kind of "Neutral Text" which existed side
by side with the Western Text; others believe that P⁷⁵-B is the
result of a revision based upon manuscripts like P⁴⁵-P⁶⁶. We see
that things have not changed very much since the time of Lake
and Streeter.

In this state of affairs it seems necessary to go into the problem
again. First of all we mean to draw attention to the corrections
in P⁶⁶. Next we want to look for the relation between ℵ B, P⁴⁵,
P⁶⁶, P⁶⁶.

In P⁶⁶ we find corrections after the scribe having made: itacisms,
leaps forward, leaps backward, omission of letters, harmonisations,
phonetic slips and nonsense readings.

The corrections are of several kinds. We find:

1. errors deleted by a) erasure
                      b) diagonal lines
                      c) dots above the word or letter

2. insertions   a) above the line
                     b) in the margin [2].

In some cases we can see clearly that the scribe corrected himself.
We find, for example, in 1, 15 that he wrote χαιχρε. This would
have been a nonsense reading. The scribe erased the letter ρ and
continued to write χραγεν. This resulted in: χαιχ.εχραγεν. Rhodes
describes this kind of correction in the following way: "In each
case the scribe has deleted an error and proceeded with a corrected
form of the text, but without any crowding of letters [3].

---

[1] R. KIEFFER, Au delà des Recensions? ... p. 222.
[2] See E. F. RHODES, "The Corrections of Papyrus Bodmer II", in:
NTS 14 1967/68, p. 271-281.
[3] RHODES, art. c., p. 272.

It is conceivable that the scribe corrected his text in accordance
with the copy he was using. This is almost certain in the case of
nonsense readings. But how are we to evaluate corrections of good
Greek readings which are also attested in the manuscripts? We
give the following examples:

3, 3. λεγω υμιν → λεγω . . . . σοι.

The word υμιν has been erased and the scribe goes on with σοι.
The reading υμιν is to be found in 597 and 713.

4, 23. In the word αυτω the letter ω has been erased and replaced
by ον. So we have the word αυτον. The word αυτω can be found in
‭ℵ‬ˣ and 124ᶜ.

10, 38. εν αυτω → εν. . τω π̄ρι. But the reading εν αυτω can be
found in *K* multi.

We can assume that the scribe corrected himself while copying
the original manuscript. But we notice that in some cases readings
have been changed which can be found in the manuscripts. Are we
to suppose that he was using another copy apart from the one he
used as a basis of his work? If we reject this idea—and I believe
that the assumption is far-fatched— we must accept that the scribe
spontaneously created variant readings which are found in other
manuscripts as well. This would mean that to draw genealogical
relations based upon common variant readings is not always a
trustworthy procedure [1].

The additions between the lines and in the margins raise further
difficulties. The scribe may have added them during his work
either from the original copy or from another copy. But they
could also have been added by a corrector from another copy.
Generally speaking it appears that the latter assumption is the
better one. The reason for this is that most corrections can be
found in de manuscripts.

Thus, we may say that a second copy has been used for the
correction of the manuscript. Before we go into the question whether
we can make out what kind of manuscript it was, we must remind
ourselves that we only know a small number of the readings in this
second copy, because we may be sure that not all the differences

---

[1] COLWELL, *Scribal Habits*, p. 370: "The dead hand of Fenton John
Anthony Hort lies heavy upon us", p. 370/1; "Hort has put genealogical
blinders on our eyes that keep us from recognizing the major role played
by scribal corruption".

between the original and the second copy have been noted in the manuscript.

All this means that research into the corrections has to be hedged with all kinds of precautions. This has not always been done. Klijn was the first one to take notice of the corrections. He showed that a number of the corrections are in agreement with the text of B. He concluded that the text of B had some authority for the corrector [1].

This is of course a conclusion which is not the whole truth. If we notice that corrections are in agreement with readings in B we can only say that the corrector has been attracted by readings in some manuscripts which are also found in B. If we are going to investigate corrections we have to ask according to what principles a corrector made his alterations and not in the first place according to which manuscript.

Birdsall had already stated that the corrections showed a tendency to smoother Greek [2]. In a later inquiry Fee concluded: "A close look at the readings of P[66c], irrespective of what other MSS have the same reading, seems roughly to suggest one principle of choice: in almost every instance the reading of P[66c] is smoother or more intelligible Greek" [3].

This conclusion is corroborated by a number of corrections of the same type. We have collected the following examples:

a) Addition of the article

1,46 φιλιππος	K A W Θ pl.	ο φιλ.	B pc.
2,25 ανθρωπου	Or	του ανθρ.	cet.
3,19 οτι	472	οτι το	cet.
3,36 αλλα	—	αλλ' η	omnes
4,12 υιοι	—	οι υιοι	omnes
6,10 ανδρες	D W fam. 1 al.	οι ανδρες	cet.
7,22 πατερων	—	των πατ.	omnes
8,25 ι̅ς̅	P[75] B 476[x]	ο ι̅ς̅	cet.
10,36 ι̅ς̅ θ̅υ̅	P[45] (vid.) ℵ W D E G al	ι̅ς̅ του θ̅υ̅	cet.
11,35 ι̅ς̅	ℵ[x]	ο ι̅ς̅	cet.
12,9 οχλος	cet.	ο οχλος	W 1010
12,12 πολυς	cet.	ο πολυς	Θ
12,16 ι̅ς̅	cet.	ο ι̅ς̅	K D W pm.
13,21 ι̅ς̅	cet.	ο ι̅ς̅	C K D Θ pl

[1] Klijn, Papyrus . . .
[3] Birdsall, The Bodmer Papyri . . . p. 13.
[2] G. D. Fee, "The Corrections of Papyrus Bodmer II and the early Textual Transmission", in: NT 7 1965, p. 247-257, p. 256.

13,23	ι̅ς̅	B	ο ι̅ς̅	cet.
18,12	υπηρεται	—	οι υπηρ.	omnes
18,40	βαραββαν	D 2145	τον βαρ.	omnes
20,30	εν βιβλιω	—	εν τω β.	omnes

b) Addition of a personal pronoun

1,22	τις	cet.	συ τις	P⁷⁵ Εx 157 c r¹ f
1,27	ειμι	P⁵ P⁷⁵ אᶜ C W al.	ειμι εγω	B K al.
1,42	ηγαγεν	cet.	ουτος ηγ.	G fam. 1 arm geo bo
2,20	και	—	και συ	omnes
3,33	μαρτυριαν	omnes	μαρτ. αυτος	—
6,52	δουναι	cet.	δουναι υμιν	U 69 483 pc.
7,37	ερχεσθω	אˣ D b e	ερχ. προς με	cet.
8,46	πιστευετε	—	πιστ. μοι	omnes
9,30	και ειπεν ο ανθρ	—	ο ανθρ. κ. ε. αυτοις	omnes
10,29	εδωκεν	—	εδωκεν μοι	omnes
14,12	μειζονα	—	μειζ. τουτων	omnes
14,14	εγω	cet.	τουτο εγω	(τουτο in P⁷⁵ B A)
14,17	γινωσκει	א B W 597 a	γιν. αυτο	K Θ pm.
18,34	τουτο	P⁶⁰ אˣ D 474 sa a aur c f ff² r¹	συ τουτο	cet.

c) Addition of a personal pronoun in the genitive with possessive significance

2,12	αδελφοι	P⁷⁵ B Ψ L pc.	αδ. αυτου	K pl.
6,60	μαθητων	—	μαθ. αυτου	omnes
11,5	αδελφην	—	αδ. αυτης	omnes
11,41	οφθαλμους	cet.	οφθ. αυτου	D 28 33 69 1241 sa bo pc.
12,26	πατηρ	cet.	πατ. μου	Θ fam. 13 pc.
12,31	κοσμου¹	D W pc.	κοσμ. τουτου	cet.
15,10	αγαπη	—	αγ. μου	omnes
15,25	νομω	—	νομ. αυτων	omnes

d) Addition of the word ουν

4,48	ειπεν	—	ειπεν ουν	omnes
4,52	ειπον	lat syˢ	ειπεν ουν	cet.
7,30	οι δε εζητουν	א	εζ. ουν	cet.
7,40	οχλου	—	οχλ. ουν	omnes
9,10	σου ηνεωχθησαν	P⁷⁵ B K pm (sed ∾)	ουν ην. σου	א C D Θ al.
10,7	ειπεν	P⁴⁵ e syˢ bo	ειπεν ουν	cet.
12,2	εποιησεν	13 syᵖᵃˡ b	επ. ουν	cet.
19,4	και εξηλθεδν (videtur)	BAL 33 al.	εξηλθουν	K W Θ pm.

The frequency of these and similar corrections leads to the conclusion that they are intentional. The witnesses to the corrected and uncorrected readings do not show any uniformity. From this list it is, therefore, absolutely impossible to gather from which kind of manuscript the corrections were made. We must further remind ourselves that many of these corrections probably have not been made with help of another manuscript and that the agreement is purely accidental [1].

This does not mean that we are completely in the dark with regard to the manuscript used by the corrector. It remains remarkable that we find a number of variant readings in the first hand which have been corrected in accordance with non-Western manuscripts. The most striking are:

2,11	πρωτην αρχην εποιησεν	q f	εποιησεν αρχην	cet.
6,64	om.	e sy^{sc}	τινες εισιν οι μη πιστευοντες	
			και	cet.
7,12	ην περι αυτου	D e	ην περι αυτου πολυς	33
8,53	οτι	D a	οστις	cet.
9,30	om. αυτοις	D b c d ff² l e	και ειπεν αυτοις	cet.
11,2	και αδελφος	D (sed και ο)	ο αδελφος	cet.
11,54	om.	sy^s	πολιν	cet.
12,3	μυρου	D b c d ff² r¹ e	μυρου ναρδου	cet.
12,16	εμνησθησαν	W b c e ff²	τοτε εμνησθησαν	cet.
12,40	μη νοησωσι	D a e f	νοησωσι	cet.
15,17	om. ινα	D e	ινα	cet.

These corrections are important because we cannot say in all cases why they were made (but cf. 9,30 and 11, 2). It is obvious that the corrector used a manuscript with less typical Western readings than were to be found in the original copy [2]. This does not mean that the manuscript was identical with, for example, P⁷⁵ of B. It might have been a manuscript like the copy of P⁷⁵ itself with readings which can be found both in Western manuscripts and in those of the B-type [3].

Even though some corrections are of the B-type we cannot

---

[1] This make us afraid to emphasize the importance of the reading ὁ προφή-της in 7, 52, cf. E. R. SMOTHERS, "The Readings in Papyrus Bodmer II", in *HTR* 51 1958, p. 109-122.

[2] Cf. Also G. D. FEE, "Codex Sinaiticus in the Gospel of John: a Contribution to Methodology in establishing textual Relationships", in: *NTS* 15 1968/69, p. 23-44, p. 44, about corrections in chapters 1-8: "the direction of correction is almost always away from D rather than toward it".

[3] RHODES, *art. c* . p. 281, supposes that the manuscript was of a "Caesarean colouring".

say that the way P⁶⁶ has been corrected shows that P-B⁷⁵ is the final development of an original "wild" text. It is impossible to conclude that P⁷⁵-B is a gradual growth. So far we have only found manuscripts with a higher or lower percentage of readings supported by D it sy or P⁷⁵-B.

Our second approach to the text of Egypt is an inquiry into the relation of ℵ, B, P⁴⁵, P⁶⁶ and P⁷⁵. All of them have the following passages: John 10, 7-25; 10, 32-11, 10; 11, 19-33 and 11, 43-56 [1]. We first looked for those passages where ℵ and B disagree.[2] Next we checked which of the three papyri supported ℵ or B. To get a clear picture we left out readings found in ℵ or B only. We also left out readings in ℵ or B which have none of the three papyri in support. This means that we are not going into the following readings:

a) Readings found only in ℵ

11,4 αλλ' ινα δοξασθη 1. om. αλλ
11,43 om. ως
11,43 εκραυγαζεν 1. εκραυγασεν

b) Readings found only in B

10,7 λεγω υμιν 1. ∽
10,23 ιησους 1. ο ιησους
10,24 εκυκλευσαν 1. εκυκλωσαν
10,25 ιησους 1. ο ιησους
10,32 πολλα εργα εδειξα υμιν καλα
11,24 εν τη αναστησει 1. εν τη αναστασει
11,52 αλλα ινα 1. αλλ' ινα

c) Readings where the three papyri do not always follow ℵ or B

10,11	ℵ	ταυτην την εντολην ελαβον	cum P⁶⁶ and P⁷⁵
	B	ταυτην εντολην ελαβον	
	P⁴⁵	ταυτην ελαβον εντολην	
10,32	ℵ	πολλα εργα καλα εδειξα υμιν	cum P⁴⁵
	B	πολλα εργα εδ. υμ. καλα	
	P⁶⁶	πολλα εδ. υμ. εργα καλα	
	P⁷⁵	πολλα καλα εργα εδ. υμ.	
10,39	ℵ	εζητουν ουν	cum P⁶⁶
	B	εζητουν	cum P⁷⁵
	P⁴⁵	εζητουν δε	
10,39	ℵ	αυτον	cum P⁴⁵
	B	παλιν αυτον	cum P⁶⁶
	P⁷⁵	αυτον παλιν	

---

[1] G. D. Fee, *Codex Sinaiticus . . .*, demonstrates the Western character of chapters 1, 1-8, 38 in ℵ. Afterwards it shows a "sudden lack of singular agreements with D" (p. 42).

[2] A list of these deviations can be found in H. C. Hoskier, *Codex B and its Allies*, Part II, London 1914.

11,22	א	αιτησει	
	B	αιτηση	cum P⁷⁵
	P⁴⁵ and P⁶⁶	αιτησης	
11,25	א	ειπεν δε	
	B	ειπεν	cum P⁴⁵ and P⁶⁶
	P⁷⁵	ειπεν ουν	

Finally we have—on this and the opposite page—43 readings where the three papyri follow א and B. These are:

		א	45	66	75	Greek	Versions
1.	10,7	ο ιησους	x	x	x	cet.	
2.		οτι		x		A D E _K_	
3.	8	om.	x		x	E F	
4.	10	ζωην αιωνιον					aeth arab
5.	11	διδωσιν	x			D	c d ff² vg
6.	12	ο δε μισθωτος		x		D X fam. 13	
7.	15	διδωμι	x	x		D W	
8.	16	ακουσωσιν				A G X	
9.	20	ελεγον ουν				D fam. 1	
10.	22	εγενετο δε	x			A X K	
11.		εν ιεροσολυμοις	x			D X fam. 1	
12.	23	σολομων . . .				A D Γ	
13.	24	om.				1241 1242	
14.		ειπον			x	1582 2193	
15.	25	απεκριθη		x		D	d r sa bo goth
16.	33	οτι				1241	c sa bo
17.	34	ο ιησους			x	cet.	
18.		εν τω νομω	x			D Θ 1170 1355	aur b c ff² l r¹ sy⁸
19.		οτι ειπα					l˟
20.	36	υιος θεου ειμι	x	x˟		D E G	
21.	38	καν εμοι μη πιστευετε				A E G	
22.		ινα γνωτε καὶ πιστευητε				A fam. 13 _K_	
23.	40	οπου				minusc.	
24.		το προτερον	x			Δ Θ fam. 13	a e ff²
25.		εμεινεν	x	x	x	cet.	
26.	41	om.				D 96 245	e c
27.	11,2	μαρια	x	x		cet.	
28.	3	προς αυτον αδελφαι				⊐ 22 249	sa bo
29.	7	ιουδαιαν					sa bo sy⁸
30.	19	μαριαν	x	x		_K_	
31.	22	οσα εαν			x	C M	
32.	24	μαρθα	x		x	A C² _K_	
33.	27	εγω πεπιστευκα	x	x	x	cet.	
34.	28	ειπουσα	x	x	x	cet.	
35.	31	μαριαν	x?	x		_K_	
36.	32	μαρια	x	x˟		D _K_	
37.	43	λαζαρ					syr
38.	44	και εξηλθεν ο τεθν.	x			_K_	
39.		αυτοις ο ιησους	x	x		cet.	
40.		υπαγειν				D _K_	
41.	50	συμφερει				D L M	
42.	54	εφρεμ				L W	
43.	56	ελεγω				D	

11,33   ℵ   εμβριμησατο τω πνευματι και εταραξεν   cum P⁷⁵
              εαυτον
        B   ενεβρ. τω πν. κ. ετ. εαυτον
      P⁴⁵ and P⁵⁶   ετ. τω πν. ως εμβριμουμενος
11,45   ℵ   πολλοι δε
        B   πολλοι ουν   cum P⁶⁶ and P⁷⁵
      P⁴⁵   πολλοι

		B	45	66	75	Greek	Versions
1.	10, 7	ιησους				118	
2.		om.	x		x	G L K	
3.	8	προ εμου		x		ℵˣ A D L W fam. 13 K	
4.	10	ζωην	x	x	x	cet.	
5.	11	τιθησιν		x	x	cet.	
6.	12	ο μισθωτος	x			G L W	
7.	15	τιθημι			x	cet.	
8.	16	ακουσουσιν	x?	x	x	K	
9.	20	ελεγον δε	x	x	x	K	
10.	22	εγενετο τοτε		x	x	L W 33	
11.		εν τοις ιεροσολυμοις		x	x	A L K	
12.	23	του σολομων . . .	x	x	x	K	
13.	24	αυτον	x	x	x	cet.	
14.		ειπε	x	x		cet.	
15.	25	απεκρ. αυτοις	x		x	cet.	
16.	33	οτι και	x	x	x	cet.	
17.	34	ιησους	x	x		W	
18.		εν τ.ν. υμων		x	x	cet.	
19.		οτι εγω ειπα	x	x	x	cet.	
20.	36	υ. του θ. ειμι		xᶜ	x	A L Θ K	
21.	38	καν εμοι μη πιστευητε	x	x	x	L K	
22.		ινα γωτε κ. γινωσκητε	x	x	x	L X W Θ fam. 1	
23.	40	εις τον τοπον οπου	x	x(ου)x		K	
24.		το πρωτον		x	x	cet.	
25.		εμενεν				21	a b c ff² l
26.	41	οτι	x	x	x	cet.	
27.	11, 2	μαριαμ			x	33	
28.	3	αι αδ. προς αυτον	x	x	x	K	
29.	7	ιουδ. παλιν	x	x	x	cet.	
30.	19	μαριαμ			x	C D L Δ	
31.	22	οσα αν	x	x		K	
32.	24	η μαρθα		x		Cˣ D L Θ	
33.	27	εγω πιστευω				47²	
34.	28	ειπασα				Cˣ	
35.	31	μαριαμ			x	Cˣ D K	
36.	32	μαριαμ		xᶜ	x	Cˣ Eˣ L 33	
37.	43	λαζαρε	x	x	x	cet.	
38.	44	εξηλθ. ο τεθν.		x	x	W Cˣ L	sa bo
39.		ιησους αυτοις			x		l vg
40.		αυτον υπαγειν	x	x	x	Cˣ L	
41.	50	συμφερει	x	x	x	K	
42.	54	εφραιμ	x	x	x	K	
43.	56	ελεγον	x	x	x	cet.	

From these 43 readings we find the following agreements:

ℵ + 45	19 ×	B + 45	24 ×
ℵ + 66	14 × (2 × 66ˣ)	B + 66	31 × (2 × 66ᶜ)
ℵ + 75	9 ×	B + 75	33 ×

These results are striking. P⁴⁵ appears to be related to ℵ and P⁷⁵ with B. P⁶⁶ is somewhere in-between, but it shows many readings supporting B[1].

The same result is gained in the following summary:

45 + 66 + 75	with ℵ	4 ×
45 + 66 + 75	with B	18 ×
45 + 66	with ℵ	7 ×
45 + 66	with B	3 ×
45 + 75	with ℵ	1 ×
45 + 75	with B	2 ×
66 + 75	with ℵ	0 ×
66 + 75	with B	8 ×

It is striking that 45 + 66 support ℵ 7 times, but that 66 + 75 do not support ℵ at all.

Next we see the papyri do not generally support in cases where the manuscript is supported by D lat sy Θ fam. 1 and fam. 13 [2]. In cases where ℵ shows "Western" readings the manuscript is supported by P⁴⁵, as in 10, 11; 10, 34 and 10, 40 or by P⁶⁶ as in 10, 15 (with P⁴⁵) and 10, 25 but *never* by P⁷⁵. B shows one "Western" reading supported by P⁷⁵ (11, 44).

Finally we see how almost all cases where ℵ and B disagree one or more of the papyri support one of these manuscripts [3].

Nobody can deny that an "Egyptian Text" existed. This text is clearly visible in P⁷⁵-B. Besides readings of the B-type we notice readings of the D-type. Most Egyptian manuscripts show a mixture of these readings. With regard to the three main papyri we see that P⁴⁵ has most Western readings and P⁷⁵ most Egyptian readings.

We cannot avoid the conclusion that in Egypt originally two types of text existed.

---

[1] See E. R. SMOTHERS, "Papyrus Bodmer II: an early Codex of St. John", in: *TS* 18 1957, p. 434-441.

[2] The same conclusion for P⁶⁶ in R. SCHIPPERS, "De Papyruscodex van Johannes (P⁶⁶)", in: *GTT* 57 1957, p. 33-45.

[3] We already find the same result in STREETER, *Four Gospels*, p. 57: "The notable fact, however, is that whenever one or more of these authorities (sc. later Egyptian texts like L C 33) desert B to give a Western reading, almost always there are others of them found ranged in support to B".

It is impossible to say which of these two types is the older.

However, we do not believe that one of these must be proved to be the older. It is conceivable that the two texts existed side by side. This would explain why these two types are still discernable in later manuscripts. It is possible and credible that the two texts where used in two different parts of the Egyptian Church. Maybe the Church was divided between a group of Christians living in the towns and an other group living in the country [1], but it is also possible that the two parts consisted of Gentile- and of Jewish-Christians.

It would be very attractive to suppose that Jewish-Christians received the Gospel and the Gospel text from Antioch or Syria. In that case we should have a very good explanation why we notice agreement between the Syriac versions and readings in Egyptian manuscripts and in particular in the Sahaidic translation.

The origin of P[75]-B is still a problem. We are, however, obliged to say that the text in these manuscripts must not be considered an uncorrupted representative of the original text in the Gentile Church of Egypt. It certainly has been revised [2]. We think that this revision was different from the revision in the Western type. The Western type was revised because it originated in a place where oral tradition was still available. This sometimes resulted in drastic rewriting and additions. In the Gentile Church one had to rely upon the written Gospels. Revision was only possible in matters of language and style.

It hardly needs to be added that the existence of these two types is the best explanation of the Caesarean Text. This text

---

[1] Cf. W. H. C. FREND, "The Gospel of Thomas: is Rehabilitation Possible?", in: *JTS* n. S. 18 1967, p. 13-26, p. 23: ". . . Christianity in Egypt presents two quite different faces. First, there is the school of Alexandria . . . On the other hand, there was the Christianity of the smaller towns and later of the Egyptian countryside . . ."

[2] The internal evidence given by K. ALAND, "Neue Neutestamentliche Papyri II", in: *NTS* 12 1965/66, p. 193-210, to show that the "Western-non-Interpolations" have to be accepted in the text of modern editions is convincing. We are, however, not able to understand that this question has received new light from the papyri, cf. E. C. COLWELL, "Hort Redivivus: A Plea and a Program", in: IDEM, "Studies in Methodology in Textual Criticism of the New Testament", in: *NTTS* IX, Leiden 1969, p. 148-171, p. 156. See also K. ALAND, "Die Bedeutung des P[75] für den Text des Neuen Testaments", in: *Studien zur Überlieferung des Neuen Testaments und seines Textes*, in: *Arbeiten zur neutestamentlichen Textforschung* II, Berlin 1967, p. 155-172.

consists of manuscripts with readings taken from the two early texts in Egypt.

If the above is true, we must say that Egypt has known no recension of the text. This means that if we were to discover a new manuscript it would be wrong to evaluate it according to its relation to one or another recension. We should have to evaluate it according to its relation to one of the two clearly distinct and original types of text in Egypt.

CHAPTER THREE

ROME, GAUL AND NORTH AFRICA

From the textbooks it appears that no unanimity exist with regard to the Old Latin version. Taylor divides the manuscripts into an African (e k), an European (a b) and an Italian (f q) text [1]. Greenlee calls the Old Latin "Itala" and speaks about the uncertainty as to whether the "Itala" represents one or several translations [2]. Metzger gives some more information and says that the Latin text has its origin in North Africa and that not long afterwards translations were made in Italy, Gaul and elsewhere [3]. All of them agree that the Old Latin version shows a Western Text. Nobody, however, goes into the questions how to explain the relation of this text to the Old Syriac. It seems as if most of the important studies which appeared before 1949 have been forgotten [4].

The best survey we know, of what happened before 1949 is by Metzger [5]. The burning question regarding the agreement between the Old Latin and the Old Syriac is clearly expounded. Some have supposed that the Old Latin version originated in Antioch and that this accounts for the agreement between the Old Latin and the Old Syriac. Others have accepted the idea that Tatian composed his Diatessaron in Rome and that this Diatessaron in its turn influenced the Syriac tetraevangelium. Finally some scholars have supposed that the Syriac Diatessaron was translated into Latin and that in this way the Latin text was influenced by genuine Syriac readings.

In the same article Metzger deals with the name "Itala". It comes from Augustine, *De Doctrina Christiana* II 15 22. Augustine speaks about a particular text of the Latin Bible, but it is absolute impossible to understand what kind of version he is referring to. For this reason we had better abandon this expression. Finally

---

[1] TAYLOR, *o.c.*, p. 27-28.
[2] GREENLEE, *Introduction*, p. 46-47.
[3] METZGER, *Text*, p. 72-75.
[4] KLIJN, *Survey*, p. 152-161.
[5] B. M. METZGER, "The Evidence of the Versions . . .", in: *New Testament Manuscript Studies*, p. 51-55.

Metzger points to the difficulty of dividing the Latin version into an European and an African text, since the representatives of the two texts show as many glaring disagreements as striking agreements among themselves.

This survey shows how many questions have yet to be solved. Therefore, it is to be regretted that during the last twenty years not many articles and books have been published on the Old Latin text of the Gospels [1]. We may be sure, however, that there will be a change in the near future. The *Vetus Latina Institut der Erzabtei Beuron* has published so many important editions of the text of the Pauline Epistles and the General Epistles and they have been accompanied by so many important studies on the text of the Epistles that we look forward with the greatest expectation to the publication of the work on the Gospels and Acts [2].

Meanwhile we cannot do more than go into what has been published on the text in the Western part of the early Christian world.

Whoever wishes to study the text of the Latin version, has also to go into the Greek text right at the beginnings of Christianity in the West. Undoubtedly the Church of Rome, Gaul and North Africa was a Greek speaking community at the beginning. This appears from such authors and writings as I Clement, Justin Martyr, Marcion and Irenaeus. Of these the text of I Clement can be left out of consideration. This means that we have to deal with the three remaining authors. Inquiry into their texts is, however, seriously hampered because all of them come from the East. Therefore, we do not know whether they show a genuine Roman text. With this reservation we must now go into recent investigations into their texts.

The text of Justin has been thoroughly investigated by Bellinzoni [3]. In his study, however, special attention has been paid to the question whether Justin used other sources apart from the canonical Gospels. Hardly anything is said about the manuscripts used by

---

[1] Of importance is that the edition of the Old Latin text of the Gospels started by JÜLICHER, continued by MATZKOW and ALAND has been completed: *Mark* 1940 (sec. ed. in preparation), *Matthew* 1938, *Luke* 1954 and *John* 1963.

[2] See VETUS LATINA INSTITUT DER ERZABTEI BEURON, *Bericht* I, Beuron/Hohenzollern 1967; *Bericht* 2 1968, and *Bericht* 3 1969, with a survey of publications on p. 4-6.

[3] BELLINZONI, *o.c.*, p. 000.

Justin. This question comes to the fore in a study by Massaux [1]. He arrives at the conclusion that the text of Justin shows a close agreement with the Latin manuscript h.

Marcion's text raises particular difficulties for us. It is known only from quotations in Tertullian's *Adv. Marcionem*. The question has been raised whether Tertullian quotes from a Latin or a Greek text. It has even been questioned whether Tertullian himself used a Latin or a Greek New Testament. At the moment the matter seems to have been settled. Higgins who again went into the problem, came to the conclusion that the quotations taken from Marcion show a clear agreement with the Old Latin usage in the European branch and the quotations taken from Tertullian's New Testament show agreement with the usage in the African branch. This seems to show that both Marcion's text as known to Tertullian and his own text were in a Latin translation [2].

Marcion's text has been thoroughly investigated by Blackman. The agreement between each individual Old Latin manuscript and Marcion is listed. The result is that Marcion does not show a particular agreement with any one Old Latin text, but the general impression is that Marcion's text belongs to the Western Text as it is manifested in the Old Latin version [3].

This is of great significance. It could be proof that Marcion used a Greek text which is the basis of the Old Latin. However, an other possibility exists: Marcion could have influenced the text of the Latin version. This very old problem has been dealt with by Blackman but he denies that Marcion exercised any extensive influence on the Latin version [4]. In addition to this we believe that this supposition is unacceptable because in the Old Latin text we do not notice any particular difference in the character of the text between Luke, the Gospel used by Marcion, and the other Gospels.

Nothing has been published about the text of Irenaeus as far as it concerns his quotations from the Gospels. With regard to the

---

[1] E. MASSAUX, "Le Texte du Sermon sur la Montagne de Matthieu utilisé par Saint Justin", in: *Ephem. Théol. Lovanienses* 28 1952, p. 411-448.

[2] A. J. B. HIGGINS, "The Latin Text of Luke in Marcion and Tertullian", in: *VC* 2 1951, p. 1-42.

[3] E. C. BLACKMAN, *Marcion and his Influence*, London 1948, p. 135-159. Blackman goes into the question whether Marcion's text shows marked agreement with the Old Latin manuscript e as has been suggested, but this idea has to be rejected.

[4] See BLACKMAN, *o.c.*, p. 157.

text of Paul, it has been shown again that the Latin translation of Irenaeus faithfully renders the original Greek text [1].

In the Western part of the Christian Church the oldest authors used a Western Text which shows a close affinity with the Old Latin version. This conclusion makes it very difficult to explain the agreement between the Old Syriac and the Old Latin from a common influence of the text of the Diatessaron only. Justin and Marcion wrote their works well before the Diatessaron was composed If, however, anyone still wishes to posit the influence of the Diatessaron on the Latin text, he has to minimise the significance of Marcion as a witness to the Western Text. In his study of the Codex Colbertinus Vogels shows himself to be an advocate of the influence of the Diatessaron on the Latin text [2]. In his "Handbuch" he says of Marcion: "Als einem 'Zeugen' für den Bibeltext können wir Marcion gegenüber gar nicht zurückhaltend genug sein" [3]. At the same time one has to avoid too great a division between the African and the European branches of the Latin version [4]. The main problem of positing a significant influence of the Diatessaron on the Latin version seems to be that this influence must be dated after the year 170. By that date a Latin translation of the New Testament must have already been in existence for some time [5].

This means that we are still looking for an acceptable explanation of the agreement between the Old Latin and the Old Syriac versions. This agreement can be traced back to the earliest days of Christian-

---

[1] K. T. SCHÄFER, "Die Zitate in der lateinischen Irenäusübersetzung und ihr Wert für die Textgeschichte des Neuen Testaments", in: *Vom Wort des Lebens*, Festschrift M. MEINERTZ, in: *Neutestam. Abhandlungen* 1. Erg. Band 1951, p. 50-59.

[2] H. J. VOGELS, "Evangelium Colbertinum", in: *Bonner Bibl. Beiträge* 4: I. *Text* and 5: II. *Untersuchungen*, Bonn 1953, p. 177.

[3] VOGELS, *Handbuch*, p. 144.

[4] VOGELS, *Evangelium Colbertinum*, p. 177. But the division seems to be an established fact, see G. W. S. FRIEDRICHSEN, "The Gothic Text of Luke in its relation to the Codex Brixianus (f) and the Codex Palatinus (e)", in: *NTS* 11 1964/65, p. 281-290, and J. MIZZI, "The Latin Text of the Gospel Quotations in St. Augustine's 'De Diversis Quaestionibus LXXXIII Liber Unus' ", in: *Augustiniana* 12 1962, p. 245-290, see also IDEM, "The Latin Text of Matt. V-VII in St. Augustine's 'De Sermone Domini in Monte' ", in: *idem* 4 1954, p. 450-494, in which it is said that Augustin's text was "a composite or mixed structure which discloses on examination undoubted traces of having undergone considerable revision under the influence of Italian and more especially European MSS" (p. 275).

[5] CHR. MOHRMANN, "Les Origines de la Latinité Chrétienne à Rome". in: *VC* 3 1949, p. 67-112 and 163-183, esp. 78-87.

ity in Rome. It might be that it has something to do with the origin of the Roman Church. This Church probably originated among Jews who were evangelised by other Jews. Did they come from Antioch? At any rate, if we look at Marcion, Justin and Irenaeus we see that these important Christians came to Rome from the East. For this reason we believe that there was ample opportunity for a text which was used in the East to have been imported into the Church of Rome.

CHAPTER FOUR

ACTS

In recent years the text of Acts has moved into the centre of interest on account of some important discoveries:

1. Codex 15 in the Cathedral of Léon (siglum: l) with a text dating from the seventh century. The parts with an Old Latin text are 8, 27-11, 13; 15, 6-12; 15, 26-38. Other parts contain a Vulgate text: 14, 21-15, 5; 15, 13-25; 15, 39-17, 25. B. Fischer who published the text came to the conclusion that the parts with an Old Latin text show some relation to the Liber Comicus (t) [1].

2. A Coptic Manuscript of the 4/5th century (siglum: cop[G67] in Epp [2], but ox 14 in the list of the Coptic New Testament Manuscripts kept by the "Institut für neutestamentliche Textforschung" [3]. From this text Pederson gave some passages in an English translation which contain Western variant readings. The text shows a remarkably close relationship to D[4].

3. A Palestinian-Syriac fragment from Khirbet Mird (siglum sy[msK] in Epp [5]), dated about 600. It contains the fragments 10, 28-29 and 32-41. It shows some agreement with D [6].

Manuscript l proves again that the Old Latin text had many Western readings. These readings are to be met with in a great number of manuscripts. They found their way from Latin into the vernacular languages of Western Europe [7]. Much more impor-

---

[1] B. FISCHER, "Ein neuer Zeuge zum Westlichen Text der Apostelgeschichte", in: *Biblical and Patristic Studies in Memory of R. P. Casey*, ed. by J. N. BIRDSALL and R. W. THOMSON, Freiburg 1963, p. 33-63.

[2] E. J. P. EPP, "The Theological Tendency of Codex Bezae Cantabrigiensis in Acts", in: *Society for New Testament Studies, Monograph Series* 3, Cambridge 1966, p. XII.

[3] E. HAENCHEN and P. WEIGANDT, "The Original Text of Acts?", in: *NTS* 14 1967/68, p. 469-481, p. 469.

[4] TH. C. PETERSEN, "An Early Coptic Manuscript of Acts: An unrevised Version of the ancient so-called Western Text", in: *CBQ* 26 1964, p. 225-241.

[5] EPP, *o.c.*, p. XII.

[6] CH. PERROT, "Un Fragment Christo-Palestinien découvert à Khirbet Mird (Actes des Apôtres X, 28-29; 32-41)", in: *RB* 79 1963, p. 506-555. An other discovery of a text of Acts has been published by R. KASSER, *Papyrus Bodmer XIII*, Bibliotheca Bodmeriana 1961, with a text like in A.

[7] A. F. J. KLIJN, "A Medieval Dutch Text of Acts", in: *NTS* 1 1954/55, p. 51-56.

tant is ox 14. This manuscript shows that there is evidence of a Western Text in Coptic. It means "that the 'western' text of the Acts of the Apostles from the fifth to the seventh centuries was known not only in Greek, Latin and Syriac, but also in the Coptic language and, therefore, in the most important *Verkehrssprachen* of the Mediterranean area" [1]. We must recall, however, that the existence of a Western Text in Egypt was already known from the papyri P[8], [29], [38], [41], [48] which contain fragments of Acts[1a]. The manuscript sy[msK] is the first discovery to demonstrate that a Western text of Acts was known in the Palestinian-Syriac language also.

For this reason the last discovery calls for our special attention. It gives us a fresh insight into the history of the text in a particular area of the Church.

The origin of the Palestinian-Syriac version "has been much disputed" [2]. As far as Acts is concerned many fragments were already known in this language before the discovery of sy[msK] [3]. These fragments, Ropes thought, were "doubtless made from the current Greek text" [4]. Duensing [5] and Black [6] who both studied a fragment (Acts 21, 14-25) of a manuscript with the title *Codex Climaci Rescriptus* published by Agnes Smith Lewis in 1909 [7], came to the conclusion that the agreement between the fragment and the Peshitto points to a relation which cannot be clearly defined. Finally, we note that Vööbus supposed the influence of an Old Syriac text on the Palestinian-Syriac [8].

---

[1] HAENCHEN-WEIGANDT, *art. c.*, p. 481.

[1a] But see P. WEIGANDT, "Zwei Griechisch-Sahidische Acta-Handschriften P[41] und 0236", in: *Materialen zur neutestamentl. Handschriftenkunde*, herausgeg. v. K. ALAND, in: *Zur neutestamentl. Textforschung*, Bd. 3, Berlin 1969, p.54-95, according to whom P[41] does not show a Western Text.

[2] See METZGER, *Text*, p. 71; B. M. METZGER, "The Evidence of the Versions for the Text of the New Testament", in: M. M. PARVIS and A. P. WIKGREN, *New Testament Manuscript Studies*, Chicago 1948, p. 25-68, p. 34, and KLIJN, *Survey*, p. 126-127.

[3] PERROT, *art. c.*, p. 544.

[4] J. H. ROPES, "The Text of Acts", in: F. J. FOAKES JACKSON and K. LAKE, *The Beginnings of Christianity* Part I, Vol. III, London 1926, p. CLXXXI.

[5] H. DUENSING, "Zwei christlich-palästinisch-aramäische Fragmente aus der Apostelgeschichte", in: *ZNW* 37 1938, p. 42-46.

[6] M. BLACK, "A Palestinian Syriac Palimpsest Leaf of Acts XXI (14-26)", in: *BJRL* 23 1939, p. 201-214.

[7] AGNES SMITH LEWIS, "Codex Climaci Rescriptus", in: *Horae Semiticae* VIII, Cambridge 1909, p. 84-101, with Acts 21, 3-14; 24, 25-26, 1 and 26, 23-27, 27.

[8] VÖÖBUS, *Early Versions . . .*, p. 130.

This last opinion Perrot considers to be corroborated by the text of sy ^{msK}. After a very learned discussion he comes to the conclusion: "Le texte du fragment ne dépend pas de la Peshitta ni de la Philoxénienne. La Peshitta et la Philoxénienne ne dépendent pas non plus du texte christo-palestinien. Le texte du fragment est plus proche du texte occidental que la Peshitta ou la Philoxénienne [1]. But Perrot also writes: "les versions syriaques, chacune à leur manière, ont des points de contact avec la version palestinienne. Ce fait postule impérieusement l'existence d'un texte de base qui explique ces multiples accords. Et ce texte fondamental doit être proche du texte occidental. N'est-ce pas le cas justement de la vieille Syriaque? [2].

In what follows we wish to go into Perrot's question. For this reason we divide the variant readings in the fragment into the following three groups:

1. The fragment is striking for its numerous singular readings:

10,28 ܩ‏ܠ‏ ܣܘ‏ ܠ‏[ܩ l. κἀμοὶ ὁ θεὸς ἔδειξεν

32 ܠܟ‏ ܘܗܘܠܝܕ l. παρὰ,

33 ܒܟܣܐ‏ ܘܡܐ l. ἐξαυτῆς οὖν

37 om. ἐκήρυξεν
38 om. ἁγίῳ
   om. πάντας
39 καὶ ἰδοὺ l. καὶ

2. The Fragment shows a great number of readings found only in sy ^{p} and sy ^{phil}:

10,28 ܐ‏ ܣܡܐ ܐ[ܩ, cf. ܣܘܡܐܣ ܐܘ ܠܡܗܕ in sy ^{p} ^{phil}

29 ܦܘ post ܘܗܘܠܝܕ cum sy ^{p} ^{phil}

33 ܘܡܐ l. οὖν, cf. ܘܡܐ in sy ^{p}

34 ... ܠܠ‏ ܩ‏ܠ‏ܠܝܕ l. οὐκ ... ὁ θεός cum sy ^{p}

37 ܘܠܐ‏ ܘܐܘ‏ l. ὑμεῖς cum sy ^{p}

38 ܣܡܩܡ‏ ܠܟ‏ l. Ἰησοῦν cum sy ^{p}

39 ܠܟܪܝܐ ܘܣܩܣܕ ... ܠܟܩ ܠܟ‏ l. Ἰησοῦν ... ἔν τε τῇ χώρᾳ cum sy ^{p}

3. All Western readings are supported by sy ^{p} except:

10,33 add. παρακαλῶν ἐλθεῖν πρὸς ἡμᾶς cum vg ^{cdd} p, sa sy ^{phil} ox 14
   add. ἐν τάχει, cum D,
34 καὶ ἀπεκρίθη ὁ πέτρος καὶ εἶπεν l. ἀνοίξας ... εἶπεν cum Ephr., comm. Acta
41 add. ἡμέρας τεσσεράκοντα cum D E sa alii Ephr

---

[1] PERROT, art. c., p. 539.
[2] PERROT, art. c., p. 540.

This means that the evidence for dependence on an Old Syriac text is not very strong. The Fragment contains a number of typical Western readings, but these are usually supported by syᵖ. We might say that this fragment shows a text like syᵖ with some more Old Syriac readings than are found in the text of the Peshitto as known to us.

This caution is required not only by the evidence of the text in the fragment, but also because of our very limited knowledge of the Old Syriac text in Syria.

The main witness of this text is Ephrem's commentary on Acts which remains only in an Armenian translation [1]. Recently this evidence has been supplemented by Kerschensteiner who collected the very small number of quotations from Acts in early Syriac writings [2].

It is interesting that three of these quotations agree with parts of the newly discovered fragment. We have already mentioned the reading 10, 35 where syᵐˢᴷ is supported by Ephrem's commentary on Acts. The other two are:

10,35 ἐν πᾶσιν ἔθνεσιν l. ἐν παντὶ ἔθνει cum syᵐˢᴷ Aphr (sed ܡ ܘܠ ܚܡܝܢܘ܀)
Ephr., *comm. Acta* et *catena* syᵖ
10,41 add. ἡμέρας τεσσεράκοντα cum syᵐˢᴷ Ephr, *comm. Diat, comm. Acta, catena* D E sa gig t vgᶜᵈᵈ

These last two readings can, however, not be considered as Old Syriac readings.

From this we might conclude that in Syria an Old Syriac text existed. It is certainly true that the text current in Syria influenced the Syro-Palestinian version. The fragment of Khirbet Mird does not, however, show with complete certainty whether it has been influenced by a pure Old Syriac text or an already revised text yet with some Old Syriac readings remaining.

Much of the research of the last twenty years has been devoted to the question whether the Western Text is a recension or whether we are only dealing with a great number of variant readings from various dates and places. This question probably arose from two important works on Acts by Ropes [3] and Clark [4]. Their results

---

[1] ROPES, *o.c.*, p. 380-453.
[2] J. KERSCHENSTEINER, "Beobachtungen zum altsyrischen Actatext", in: *Bibl.* 45 1964, p. 63-74.
[3] ROPES, *o.c.*
[4] A. C. CLARK, *The Acts of the Apostles*, Oxford 1933.

were totally different. Ropes almost completely rejected the Western
Text [1] while Clark completely accepted it. From this it seemed
that one was obliged to consider the Western Text as an entity
which had to be taken or rejected as a whole.

Ropes, however, was not quite clear in his ideas about the
origin of the Western Text in Acts. He does not offer a choice
between "a recension" and "an accumulation of micellaneous
variants". Although he speaks of a recension it is one spread over a
period of "fifty years after the book passed into circulation" [2].
One wonders if it is still possible to speak of a "definite rewriting" in
these circumstances. One should rather speak of a period in which
it was still possible for "wild texts" to come into being. But in
spite of this Ropes believed "that a definite 'Western' text whether
completely recoverable in its original form or not, once actually
existed" [3]. He goes further and says: "the 'Western' text, once
produced, was liable to modification and enlargement" [4]. This
raises the questions how we can distinguish between the "modification" and the original "rewriting" and what is the difference
between a "rewriting" over a period of fifty years, as Ropes
supposed, and "later modifications".

The problem could be solved if we only possessed a manuscript
with a "pure" or "homogeneous" Western Text. An other way to
solve the problem would be by looking for one leading tendency
in the Western Text which clearly shows that the variant readings
originated in one basic viewpoint.

Everyone agrees that the first possibility is out of the question.
A "pure" Western Text does not exist. The main representative
of this Text, Codex D, is itself a "mixed text". It is to be regretted
that Pederson was led to believe that ox 14 showed the original
Western Text as he stated in the title of his article on this manuscript: "An early Coptic Manuscript of Acts: An unrevised Version
of the ancient so-called Western Text" [5].

Epp fastened on this title and said: "a full assessment of cop^{G67}

---

[1] Ropes accepted the Western readings in 20, 15; 21, 1 and 27, 5.
[2] ROPES, *o.c.*, p. VIII.
[3] ROPES, *o.c.*, p. VIII.
[4] ROPES, *o.c.*, p. VIII.
[5] Petersen has some strange ideas about the history of the text. He
speaks of the Western "recension" which "was all but universally displaced
by the revised text of the neutral and Alexandrian recension", see *art. c.*,
p. 226.

should shed at least some light on the longstanding question of the homogeneity of the Western text" [1]. In order to answer the question he compared the Coptic manuscript with D. One positive result stands out clearly: some readings formerly known only in D and thus suspected of being introduced by the scribe of D, are supported by ox 14. They appear to be "real" Western readings. Also some readings in Western witnesses with a mixed text are supported by ox 14. But this means no more than that a few readings can no longer be called "singular". At the same time the number of singular readings has been increased because some are now to be found in ox 14 only. Epp says that of the "some 250 variation-units" in ox 14 "40 to 50 are unique". Epp is justified in asking "can a revision (or better, a recension) tolerate this ratio of unique readings and still be a recension?" [2].

About two years later Haenchen and Weigandt investigated the text of ox 14 again [3]. They criticize the words of Petersen that ox 14 is "the earliest completely preserved and entirely unadulterated witness of the Western text". According to Haenchen and Weigandt even ox 14 is a "mixed text". They point to 2, 41:

D πιστεύσαντες
cet. ἀποδεξάμενοι τὸν λόγον
ox 14 (and sy[hcl]): . . . who received his word in gladness and believed, were . . .

This reading shows that even ox 14 has been influenced by both the Western and the Egyptian Text. Next they point to the corrections in Old Testament quotations which show that they were made according to a Coptic translation of the Old Testament.

However, it is still premature to say a final word with regard to ox 14 since the text has still to be published. But we can say already that even ox 14 is not a "pure" Western text of Acts. This means at the same time that we doubt whether such a "pure" Western Text ever existed.

Another approach to the problem is by an investigation into the character of the variant readings in the Western Text. The first step in this field was taken by Menoud in 1951. He pointed

---

[1] E. J. EPP, "Coptic Manuscript G 67 and the Rôle of Codex Bezae as a Western Witness in Acts", in: *JBL* 85 1966, p. 197-212.
[2] EPP, *art. c.*, p. 212.
[3] HAENCHEN and WEIGANDT, *art. c.*

to anti-Jewish remarks, the emphasis on universalism, frequent mentioning of the Spirit and alterations in the name of Jesus [1]. This work has been continued, along different lines sometimes, by Epp [2], Thiele [3], Hanson [4] and Wilcox [5].

In these studies one points to particular tendencies which have caused the variant readings in the Western Text. It appears that hardly anything has been added to the list given by Menoud. Only Wilcox pointed to Semitisms in the Western Text [6]. If we leave this out of consideration we must say that these tendencies do not point to a particular time or a particular place. They are to be expected in texts where scribes where free to make alterations. Epp realized this difficulty and for that reason he looked only for anti-Judaic tendencies in Codex D. He rightly states: "If the present study of Codex Bezae in Acts is to contribute to knowledge of the 'Western' text as a whole, it is necessary, as previously stated, to differentiate between readings which can reasonably be assumed to be ancient and part of the genuine 'Western' tradition and those which may have come into the tradition at a later time—in some cases perhaps at a date almost as recent as the date of Codex Bezae itself" [7]. Of course, It still has to be proved that a "genuine" Western Text existed. According to Epp a genuine Western reading has to be supported by D it sy [8]. Epp, however, does not work with this criterion. He keeps to the readings on D. This,

---

[1] P. H. MENOUD, "The Western Text and the Theology of Acts", in: *Studiorum Novi Testamenti Societas*, Bulletin II 1951, p. 19-32.

[2] E. J. EPP, "The 'Ignorance Motif' in Acts and Anti-Judaic Tendencies in Codex Bezae", in: *HTR* 55 1962, p. 51-62, and IDEM, *The Theological Tendency* . . .; see *Review* by R. P. C. HANSON, "The Ideology of Codex Bezae in Acts", in: *NTS* 4 1967/68, p. 282-286, and R. P. MARKHAM, in: *The Bible Translator* 19 1968, p. 189-191.

[3] W. THIELE, "Ausgewählte Beispiele zur Charkterisierung des 'West-lichen' Textes der Apostelgeschichte", in: *ZNW* 56 1965, p. 51-63.

[4] R. P. C. HANSON, "The Provenance of the Interpolator in the 'Western' Text of Acts and of Acts itself", in: *NTS* 12 1965/66, p. 211-230, and IDEM, *The Ideology* . . .

[5] M. WILCOX, *The Semitisms in Acts*, Oxford 1965.

[6] WILCOX, arrives at the same conclusion as BLACK, *Aramaic Approach*. . ., viz. that Semitisms were "confined to one manuscript or group of manu-scripts, frequently D (and its allies)". He also points to the difficulty of this phenomenon because here "primitive material can have survived unrevised (although we must remember that some such Semitisms may be due to Semitic-thinking scribes)", see p. 185.

[7] EPP, *Tendency*, p. 27.

[8] EPP, *Tendency*, p. 28.

however, meant that his conclusions are very cautious. He says that his study "admittedly leaves unanswered many of the traditional text-critical questions regarding the 'western text' " [1].

Epp's study was cautiously limited. Hanson draws much more general conclusions from the variant readings. He notices that readings show a tendency to make the text clearer. He does not like to say that all those improvements are the work of an interpolator, but they are "a single phenomenon" [2]. He rightly says that the Western Text "may indeed be composite and contain contributions made by several textual traditions" [3]. But this again does not prevent Hanson from speaking about an "interpolator" who tried "to bring its (sc. Acts) thought into line with the thought of his day and milieu" [4].

We believe that Hanson wishes to emphasize the homogeneity of the Western Text in Acts. This appears from his supposition that the interpolator lived in Rome. He gives three reasons for this:

a) D magnifies the part of Peter. This comes to the fore in readings like I, 23 ἔστησεν δύο l. ἔστησαν δύο cum D-gig and II, 1-2 διὰ ἱκανοῦ χρόνου ἠθέλησε πορευθῆναι l. ἀνέβη D sy^{ncl} ox 14.

Already J. H. Crehan had pointed to the important place of Peter [5]. Epp, however, believed that "it is easier to see in the D-text an intention to stress the importance of the apostles in general" [6].

b) D shows that the interpolator was surprisingly well informed about the family of the Herods. Hanson points to 24, 27 with the reading: ἐν τηρήσει διὰ Δρύσιλλαν in 614 2147 sy^{hcl}.

Hanson agrees that these proofs are "faint and uncertain" [7], but the matter is settled by

c) 28, 16 ὁ ἑκατόναρχης παρέδωκεν τοὺς δεσμίους τῷ στρατοπεδάρχῳ

According to Hanson we have here a technical term which "creates a strong presumption that the man who wrote it was well acquainted with the different functions of the officers of the Praetorian Guards at Rome" [8].

---

[1] EPP, *Tendency*, p. 171.

[2] HANSON, *Provenance*, p. 216.

[3] HANSON, *Provenance*, p. 217.

[4] HANSON, *Ideology*, p. 286.

[5] J. CREHAN, "Peter according to the D-Text of Acts", in: *JTS* n. S. 18 1957, p. 596-603.

[6] EPP, *Tendency*, p. 163.

[7] HANSON, *Provenance*, p. 222.

[8] HANSON, *Provenance*, p. 223.

Thus we see that finally Hanson's idea only rests on one reading.

One wonders whether this is enough to argue that the Western interpolator lived in Rome, especially because this last reading is not specifically Western. It is found in some Western witnesses and also in the Byzantine Text.

The riddle of the Western Text in Acts has not been solved. We do not believe that anyone succeeded in finding a "pure" or "original" Western Text. And the reason is that such a text did not exist. Western readings are spread over a number of manuscripts and they probably originated in a number of places over a number of years. This, however, does not mean that all these studies which tried to go into this subject, were in vain. On the contrary, it is once again shown that the Western readings are very old and many are of a particular significance. In a great many cases they are deliberate alterations [1]. This means that they are recognizable and that many can be rejected as a whole when we try to discover the original text. Haenchen in particular pointed to variant readings in the Western Text which can be grouped together [2].

All this, however, does not make the recovery of the original text of Acts an easier task. Just because we concluded that the Western Text is not a clear cut recension, so we have to judge each separate reading on its merits [3]. The eclectic method for Acts propagated

---

[1] This generally accepted view can be found in modern commentaries like E. HAENCHEN, "Die Apostelgeschichte", in: *Krit.-Exeg. Komm. ü.d.N. T.*, Göttingen 1961[13], p. 47-53, and H. CONZELMANN, "Die Apostelgeschichte", in: *Handb. z. N.T.* 7, Tübingen 1963, p. 2-3. Only P. GLAUE, "Der älteste Text der geschichtlichen Bücher des Neuen Testaments", in: *ZNW* 45 1954, p. 90-108, tried to defend the Western Text, but he was criticised by E. HAENCHEN, "Zum Text der Apostelgeschichte", in: *ZTK* 44 1957, p. 22-55, esp. 30-35.

[2] E. HAENCHEN, "Schriftzitate und Textüberlieferung in der Apostelgeschichte", in: *ZTK* 51 1954, p. 153-167, criticizing the more eclectic method of L. CERFAUX, "Citations scripturaires et Tradition textuelle dans le Livre des Acts", in: *Mél. M. Goguel*, Neuchâtel-Paris 1950, p. 43-51, also in "Recueil L. Cerfaux II, in: *Bibl. Eph. Theol. Lovan.* vol. VII, Gembloux 1954, p. 93-101.

[3] See for example C. D. F. MOULE, "H. W. Moule on Acts IV 25", in: *ET* 65 1953/54, p. 220-221; J. DUPLACY, "A Propos d'une Variante 'occidentale' des Actes des Apôtres (iii 11)", in: *Rev. des Études Augustiniennes* 2 1956, p. 231-242, and J. DUPONT, "La Mission de Paul à Jérusalem (Acts xii 25)", in: *NT* 1 1956, p. 275-303.

[4] C. S. C. WILLIAMS, "A Commentary on the Acts of the Apostles", in: *Black's New Testament Commentary*, London 1957, p. 49.

by Williams [4], Dupont [5] and Kilpatrick [6] seems to be the right procedure to restore the original text. Admitting the soundness of this procedure we nevertheless have to say that this method arrives at such varying results that we wonder whether editors of Greek texts and translations can safely follow this road [1]. The subjective element seems to play too great a part as soon as we have to judge variant readings on internal grounds alone [2].

---

[5] J. DUPONT, "Les Problèmes des Actes d'après les Travaux récents", in: *Anal. Lovan. Bibl. et Orient.*, Ser. II, Fasc. 17, Louvain 1950, p. 26.

[6] G. D. KILPATRICK, "An eclectic Study of the Text of Acts", in: *Bibl. and Patristic Studies ... R. P. Casey*, p. 64-77.

[1] Cf. A. F. J. KLIJN, "In Search of the Original Text of Acts", in: *Studies in Luke-Acts, Essays presented in honor of P. Schubert*, ed. by L. E. KECK and J. L. MARTYN, Nashville 1966, p. 103-110.

[2] The next step is the introduction of conjectures again, as argued by M. DIBELIUS, "Der Text der Apostelgeschichte", in: M. DIBELIUS, *Aufsätze zur Apostelgeschichte*, Göttingen 1951, p. 76-83, criticized by A. D. NOCK, "Review Dibelius, Aufsätze ...", in: *Gnomon* 25 1953, p. 497-506, p. 502.

CHAPTER FIVE

THE WESTERN TEXT

It is still customary to divide manuscripts into the four well known families: the Alexandrian, the Caesarean, the Western and the Byzantine.

This classical division can no longer be maintained. This has been shown by such manuscripts as P^{45} and P^{66} which can not be assigned to any of these texts. It is said that these manuscripts show a distinct common character with Western and Alexandrian readings more or less equally distributed over their text, but this very character makes it impossible to fit them into either the Western or the Alexandrian family.

A second drawback of this division is that manuscripts are classified according to a supposed geographical origin. This goes back to a time when one supposed that local texts were based on local recensions. Now we know that each separate region had its own individual history and that in that history drastic recensions did not play any part. All changes are the result of a gradual development.

If any progress is to be expected in textual criticism we have to get rid of the division into local texts. New manuscripts must not be allotted to a geographically limited area but to their place in the history of the text.

In this history we notice the following stages:

1. The most ancient witnesses to the Gospel tradition are the Apostolic Fathers and the Apologists. Their text shows that in their time oral and written tradition were used side by side. Oral and written tradition, written and written tradition and oral and oral tradition were freely combined and harmonised. This followed a pattern known from the beginning of Christian tradition. It is this pattern followed by Matthew when he combined and harmonised Markan and other traditions to make a new "life of Jesus".

From the Apostolic Fathers and later authors we see that this genuine Christian way of dealing with traditional material did not come to an end once the canonical Gospels had been written. It

was continued, now with help of these written Gospels. The extent
of this work depended on the quantity of oral traditional matter
and the importance which was attached to it. We may assume that
very old christian communities with venerable and ancient traditions would be more inclined to preserve these traditions than a
Church which heard the Gospel after the written Gospels had
already become more or less the only authority in matters of
Gospel tradition. This means that generally speaking the very
old Jewish-Christian communities must have possessed the oldest
traditions.

In communities with a venerable treasure of Gospel tradition
written Gospels were bound to be influenced by that tradition.
And even if they were not directly influenced by that tradition,
the written Gospels would not be held in the same esteem in these
places as in places where they were the only source of Gospel
tradition. But this did not always happen in the same way. We
may ask how long one can go on adding traditional material
before it can no longer be recognized as the original Gospel. The
author of Matthew for example, added so much to Mark that
we speak about a new Gospel. In its turn the same happened in
Matthew which was worked up in such a way that later ecclesiastical
authors spoke of the resulting writings as Jewish-Christian Gospels.
But there are a lot of possibilities between a rewriting as found in
the Jewish-Christian Gospels and some simple additions to the
original draft.

We can be sure that in particular parts of the Church this work
of adapting, combining, rewriting and harmonising went on for a
long time. We might even go so far as to argue that Tatian's
Diatessaron is the climax of this process. This might be called the
last effort to combine disparate Gospel tradition into one writing.
In other parts of the Church, however, this way of dealing with
tradition was resisted: the fourfold Gospel was accepted as the
way in which the Gospel tradition had to be accepted.

In communities where no venerable tradition existed the written
Gospel escaped from the rewriting we have described above.

We do not possess Gospel manuscripts dating from this period
which lasted in Edessa till about 150. But this does not mean that
numerous readings in later manuscripts do not reflect this original
state of affairs. We only have to point to the agreement between
Justin and the Old Latin, Marcion and D, to readings found in the

Diatessaron, the Old Latin and the Old Syriac. All these witnesses of course differ in many ways, but just for this reason we are repeatedly struck by their equally many agreements.

At the present time we know that readings in this group of witnesses are of the same antiquity as readings found in P75-B. We have drawn the conclusion that we are dealing with two clearly different texts of Egypt. The P75-B text must have come to Egypt at a very early date and at a time before it could be influenced in such thorough way as the "Western Text".

Going back to the text we meet in D, the Old Latin and the other witnesses we call "Western", we notice that agreement is sometimes striking. We cannot explain this agreement by the influence of Tatian. "Western" readings are known long before Tatian, as we learned from the Gospel of Thomas. Their origin must go further back into history and it must be looked for in a particular centre of Christianity. Otherwise it is impossible to understand how similar readings can be found in the East and in the West, Rome, Edessa and Egypt.

We cannot suppose any other place than Antioch as the origin of these readings. Antioch must have had a venerable treasure of tradition. Here we may suppose a Jewish-Christian community where Gospel tradition was handed down. Here we have a town which could have had relations with a place like Edessa. It is from this town that we may suppose that Christianity was brought to the Jewish communities in Rome and Alexandria. We can easily imagine Antioch as a melting-pot of Gospel tradition and as a distributor of expanded Gospels.

2. The second stage in the history of the text is the period in which the Church accepted virtually only the four Gospels. We earlier pointed to Edessa as one place where this happened only at a later date. During this period we notice a rapid influence of one text upon another. This is clearly to be seen in Egypt where the "P75-B Text" was influenced by the "Western Text" and the other way round so as to produce such texts as P45, P66, and numerous other mixed texts. During this time the Syriac Diatessaron was translated into Latin introducing a fresh source of corruption into the Latin version of the Gospels. It was the time when secondary translations were made like the Armenian and Georgian based upon Syriac and Greek Gospel texts. This is the time when a tetraevange-lium was introduced in Edessa from the West.

During this time many typical additions, found in the original text of Antioch, must have been corrected in accordance with a text like in P^{75}-B. This did not happen because people knew that the latter text was "better", but only because it was a text of the Gentile Christians whose influence was growing more and more at the expense of the Jewish Christians.

3. The third stage in the history of the text shows an intensified work on the text. Gradual, but persistent work on this text resulted in the Vulgate, the Peshitto and the Byzantine Text.

This reconstruction of the history of the text does not raise any problems for us. It is obvious that textual corruption started right after the autographs had been completed. For, the Gospels were written in a region where Gospel tradition was well known and this tradition will have influenced the written Gospels.

More difficult is the existence of a text like P^{75}-B. It is impossible to imagine that this text was made from a Western manuscript. The text can only be explained if we accept that it has been withdrawn from the influence of oral Gospel tradition at a very early date.

From all this it is clear that it is very difficult to decide whether a quotation in an early writing which has a parallel in the New Testament has been drawn from the oral tradition or from the New Testament. We may even say that in the light of textual history the question does not even arise because a clear-cut division between written and oral tradition was not made. In certain regions the same applies to the division between what we call apocryphal and canonical Gospels. The so-called Jewish-Christian Gospels must have gradually grown out of the conflation of oral and written tradition.

Again we are not justified in speaking of Jewish-Christian Gospel tradition whenever we are referring to oral tradition. We certainly agree that much of the oral tradition circulated among Christians who belonged to the Jewish people. But that was not because they were Jews but because the further we go back into history of the Church the more we are brought face to face with the Jewish origin of Christianity. Therefore, we do better to speak of early Christian oral tradition.

Then we have to decide in what way we should evaluate manuscripts and quotations [1]. If we are dealing with late witnesses it remains

---

[1] See E. C. COLWELL, "The Significance of Grouping of New Testament Manuscripts", in: *NTS* 4 1957/58, p. 73-92; IDEM, "Method in Locating a

advisable to make a collation against the textus receptus or, if we are dealing with versions, against the Vulgate or the Peshitto. Early manuscripts and quotations must be collated against P⁷⁵-B. This is, as we know, a text which escaped the "Western" peculiarities and it is a text which is partially responsible for many mixed texts. After such a collation we shall not be able to say more than that a manuscript is more or less related to P⁷⁵-B. Readings which disagree with P⁷⁵-B can be compared with manuscripts like the Old Syriac, the Old Latin and the Diatessaron.

Finally it is necessary to say something about the reconstruction of the original text. As far as we know, textual history does not offer us any evidence that one manuscript or type of text shows the original text. We may say that P⁶⁵-B escaped an important amount of corruption, but that does not mean that it has not been corrupted at all. As we stated above [1], it is conceivable that P⁷⁵-B has been linguistically corrected. Particularly in cases where we have to choose between a "Semitism" in the "Western" witnesses and a good Greek reading in P⁷⁵-B we probably aught to follow the "Western" reading. The same applies in cases where P⁷⁵-B shows atticisms. On the other hand harmonisations and additions to make intelligible reading in the Western Text have to be rejected. This means that we have to judge readings on internal considerations, but without neglecting the origin of the different manuscripts. We believe that the present alternative between "the eclectic method" and the following of a particular "good" manuscript or text is a fallacy. The "eclectic method" would need to be followed only if we did not know anything of the history of the text. But we do know something about these things and we know what influences come to bear upon the manuscripts and the groups of manuscripts because of their historical background. This we have to take into account when we choose a particular reading.

---

newly discovered Manuscript within the Manuscript Tradition of the Greek New Testament", in: *Studia Evangelica*, in: *TU* 73 1959, p. 757-777; IDEM, "The Origin of Text-Types of New Testament Manuscripts", in: *Early Christian Origins, Mélanges Willoughby*, ed. A. WIKGREN, Chicago 1962, p. 128-136; E. C. COLWELL-E. W. TUNE, "The quantitative Relationships between MS Text-Types", in: *Bibl. and Patrist. Stud. ... R. P. Casey*, p. 25-32; IDEM, "Variant Readings. Classification and Use", in: *JBL* 83 1964, p. 253-261.

[1] See p. 49.

BIBLIOGRAPHY

L. Abramowski-A. F. Goodman, "Luke XIII. 46 ΠΑΡΑΤΙΘΜΑΙ in a rare Syriac rendering", in: *NTS* 13 1966/67, p. 290-291.

K. Aland, "The present Position of New Testament Textual Criticism, in: *Studia Evangelica*, in: *TU* 73 1959, p. 717-131.

——, "Eine Bemerkung zur gegenwärtigen Arbeit der neutestamentlichen Textkritik", in: *BZ* n.F.4 1960, p. 315-318.

——, "Neue Neutestamentliche Papyri II', in: *NTS* 9 1962/63, p. 303-316.

——, "Neue Neutestamentliche Papyri II", in: *NTS* 10 1963/64, p. 62-79.

——, "Neue Neutestamentliche Papyri II", in: *NTS* 11 1964/65, p. 1-21.

——, "The Significance of the Papyri for Progress in New Testament Research", in: *The Bible in Modern Scholarship*, edited by J. Th. Hyatt, Nashville, New York 1965, p. 325-346.

——, "Neue Neutestamentliche Papyri II", in: *NTS* 12 1965/66, p. 193-210.

——, Die Bedeutung des P75 für den Text des Neuen Testaments", in: *Studien zur Überlieferung des Neuen Testaments und seines Textes*, in: *Arbeiten zur neutestamentlichen Textforschung* II, Berlin 1967, p. 155-172.

——, "Bemerkungen zu Probezeiten einer groszen kritischen Ausgabe des Neuen Testaments", in: *idem*, p. 81-90, cf. *NTS* 12 1966, p. 176-185.

——, "The Greek New Testament: its present and future Editions", in: *JBL* 87 1968, p. 179-186.

Tj. Baarda, "The Gospel Text in the Biography of Rabulla", in: *VC* 14 1960, p. 102-127.

——, "Op Zoek naar de Tekst van het Diatessaron", in: *VT* 32 1961/62, p. 107-119.

——, "A Syriac Fragment of Mar Ephraem's Commentary on the Diatessaron", in: NTS 8 1961/62, p. 287-300.

——, "Dionysius Bar Salībī and the Text of Luk. I. 35", in: *VC* 17 1963, p. 225-229.

A. Baker, "Pseudo-Macarius and the Gospel of Thomas", in: *VC* 18 1964, p. 215-225.

——, "The Gospel of Thomas and the Diatessaron", in: *JTS* n.S. 16 1965, p. 449-454.

——, "The 'Gospel of Thomas' and the Syriac 'Liber Graduum' ", in: *NTS* 1965/66, p. 49-55.

——, "The Significance of the New Testament Text of the Syriac Liber Graduum", in: *Studia Evangelica* V, in: *TU* 103 1968, p. 171-175.

——, "Syriac and the Scriptural Quotations of Pseudo Macarius", in: *JTS* n. S. 20 1969, p. 133-149.

L. W. Barnard, "The Origin and Emergence of the Church in Edessa during the first two Centuries A.D.", in: *VC* 22 1968, p. 151-175.

J. W. B. Barns, "Papyrus Bodmer II, Some Corrections and Remarks", in: *Le Muséon* 75 1962, p. 327-329.

H.-W. Bartsch, "Das Thomas-Evangelium und die synoptischen Evangelien", in: *NTS* 6 1959/60, p. 249-261.

J. B. Bauer, "Sermo Peccati. Hieronymus und das Nazarenerevangelium", in: *BZ* n.F. 4 1963, p. 122-128.

A. Bellinzoni, "The Sayings of Jesus in the Writings of Justin Martyr", in: *Supplem. to NT* XVII 1967.

J. N. Birdsall, "The Text of the Gospels in Photius", in: *JTS* n.S. 7 1956, p. 42-55 and 190-198.

J. N. Birdsall, "Photius and the Text of the Fourth Gospel", in: *NTS* 4 1957/58, 61-63.
——, *The Bodmer Papyri of the Gospel of John*, London 1960.
——, "The Syriac Original of the Commentary of Ephrem the Syrian upon the Concordant Gospel", in: *The Evangelical Quarterly* 37 1965, p. 132-141.
M. Black, "Rabulla and the Peshitta", in: *BJRL* 33 1950, p. 203-210.
——, "The Gospel Text of Jacob of Serug", in: *JTS* n.S. 2 1951, p. 57-63.
——, "Zur Geschichte des Syrischen Evangelientextes", in: *TL* 77 1952, c. 705-710.
——, The Text of the Peshitta Tetraevangelium", in: *Studia Paulina* in hon. J. de Zwaan, Haarlem 1953, p. 20-27.
——, *An Aramaic Approach to the Gospels and Acts*, Oxford 1967³.
E. C. Blackman, *Marcion and his Influence*, London 1948.
R. P. Blake and M. Brière, "The Old Georgian Version of the Gospels with the Variants of the Opiza and Tbet' Gospels. Edited with a Latin Translation", in: *Patrol Orient.*. 26, 4, Paris 1950.
M.-E. Boismard, "A Propos de Jean V, 39. Essai de Critique Textuelle", in: *RB* 55 1948, p. 5-34.
——, „Critique Textuelle et Citations Patristiques", in: *RB* 57 1950, p. 381-408.
——, "Lectio Brevior Potior", in: *RB* 58 1951, p. 161-168.
——, "Problèmes de Critique Textuelle concernant la quatrième Évangile"; in: *RB* 60 1953, p. 347-371.
——, "Le Papyrus Bodmer II", in: *RB* 64 1957, p. 362-398.
——, "Papyrus Bodmer II. Supplément . . . 1962", in: *RB* 70 1962, p. 120-133.
B. Botte, "Un Témoin du Texte Césaréen de quatrième Évangile: l 253", in: *Mél. Bibl. A. Robert*, Travaux de l'Institut Cath. de Paris 4 1956, p. 466-469.
L. Cerfaux, "Citations scripturaires et Tradition textuelle dans le Livre des Actes", in: *Mél. M. Goguel*, Neuchâtel-Paris 1950, p. 43-51, also in "Recueil L. Cerfaux" II, in: *Bibl. Eph. Theol. Lovan.* vol. VII, Gembloux 1954, p. 93-101.
K. W. Clark, "The Effect of recent Textual Criticism upon the New Testament Studies", in: D. W. Davies and D. Daube, *The Background of the New Testament . . .* in hon. of C. H. Dodd, Cambridge 1956, p. 21-51.
——, "The Text of the Gospel of John in third-century Egypt", in: *NT* 5 1962, p. 17-24.
E. C. Colwell, "The Significance of Grouping of New Testament Manuscripts", in *NTS* 4 1957/58, p. 73-92.
——, "Method in Locating a newly discovered Manuscript within the Manuscript Tradition of the Greek New Testament", in: *Studia Evangelica*, in: *TU* 73 1959, p. 757-777.
——, "The Origin of Texttypes of New Testament Manuscripts", in: *Mél. Willoughby*, ed. A. Wikgren, Chicago 1961, p. 128-138.
——, "Scribal Habits in early Papyri. A Study in the Corruption of the Text", in: *The Bible in Modern Scholarship*, ed. by J. Ph. Hyatt, Nashville-New York 1965, p. 350-389.
——, "External Evidence and the New Testament Textual Criticism", in: *Studies in the History and Text of the New Testament* in honor of K. W. Clark by B. L. Daniels and M. J. Suggs, in: S and D XXIX, Salt Lake City 1967, p. 1-12.

E. C. COLWELL, "Studies in Methodology in Textual Criticism of the New Testament", in: *NTTS* IX, Leiden 1969.

E. C. COLWELL, I. A. SPARKS, F. WISSE, P. R. McREYNOLDS, "The International Greek New Testament Project: a Status Report", in: *JBL* 87 1968, p. 187-197.

E. C. COLWELL and E. W. TUNE, "The quantitative Relationships between MS Text Types", in: *Biblical and Patristic Studies* in memory of R. P. CASEY, ed. J. N. BIRDSALL and R. W. THOMSON, Freiburg 1963, p. 25-32.

E. C. COLWELL and E. W. TUNE, "Variant Readings. Classification and Use", in: *JBL* 83 1964, p. 253-261.

O. CULLMANN, "Das Thomasevangelium und die Frage nach dem Alter der in ihm enthaltenen Tradition", in: *TL* 85 1962, c. 321-334.

M. DIBELIUS, "Der Text der Apostelgeschichte", in: *Aufsätze zur Apostelgeschichte*, Göttingen 1951, p. 76-83.

J. DUPLACY, "A Propos d'une Variante 'occidentale' des Actes des Apôtres (iii 11)", in: *Rev. des Étud. August.* 2 1956, p. 231-242.

——, "Où en est la Critique Textuelle du Nouveau Testament?", in: *RSR* 45 1957, p. 419-441.

——, "Bulletin de Critique Textuelle du Nouveau Testament", in: *RSR* 50 1962, p. 242-263, 564-598; 51 1963, p. 432-462.

——, "Bulletin de Critique Textuelle du Nouveau Testament II", in: *RSR* 53 1965, p. 257-284 and 54 1966, p. 426-476.

——, "Une Tâche importante en Difficulté: l'Édition du Nouveau Testament en Grec", in: *NTS* 14 1967/68, p. 457-468.

J. DUPONT, "Les Problèmes des Actes d'après les Travaux récents", in: *Anal. Lovan. Bibl. et Orient.*, Sér. II, Fasc. 17. Louvain 1950.

——, "La Mission de Paul à Jérusalem (Act xii 25)", in: *NT* 1 1956, p. 275-303.

E. J. EPP, "The 'Ignorance Motif' in Acts and Anti-Judaic Tendencies in Codex Beza", in: *HTR* 55 1962, p. 51-62.

——, "Coptic Manuscript G67 and the Rôle of Codex Bezae as a Western Witness in Acts", in: *JBL* 85 1966, p. 197-212.

——, "The Theological Tendency of Codex Bezae Cantabrigiensis in Acts", in: *Society for New Testament Studies, Monograph Series* 3, Cambridge 1966.

E. FASCHER, *Textgeschichte als hermeneutisches Problem*, Halle 1953.

G. D. FEE, "The Corrections of Papyrus Bodmer II and the early Textual Transmission", in: *NT* 7 1965, p. 247-257.

——, "Codex Sinaiticus in the Gospel of John: a Contribution to Methodology in establishing textual Relationships", in: *NTS* 15 1968/69, p. 23-44.

B. FISCHER, "Ein neuer Zeuge zum Westlichen Text der Apostelgeschichte", in: *Biblical and Patristic Studies* in Memory of R. P. CASEY, ed. by J. N. BIRDSALL and R. W. THOMSON, Freiburg 1963, p. 33-63.

J. A. FITZMYER, "Papyrus Bodmer II: Some Features of our oldest Text of Luke", in: *CBQ* 24 1962, p. 170-179.

W. H. C. FREND, "The Gospel of Thomas: is Rehabilitation Possible?", in: *JTS* n.S. 18 1967, p. 13-26.

G. W. S. FRIEDRICHSEN, "The Gothic Text of Luke in its relation to the Codex Brixianus (f) and the Codex Palatinus (e)", in: *NTS* 11 1964/65, p. 281-290.

G. GARITTE, "L'Ancienne Version Géorgienne des Actes des Apôtres", in: *Bibl. du Muséon* 38, Louvain 1955.

B. Gärtner, *The Theology of the Gospel according to Thomas*, New York 1961.

T. Gaumer, "An Examination of some Western textual Variants adopted in the Greek Text of the New English Bible", in: *The Bible Translator* 16 1965, p. 184-189.

J. C. L. Gibson, "From Qumran to Edessa or the Aramaic-speaking Church before and after 70 A.D.", in: *The Annual of the Leeds Univ. Oriental Society* V 1963-1965.

J. F. Glasson, "An early Revision of the Gospel of Mark", in: *JBL* 85 1966, p. 231-233.

P. Glaue, "Der älteste Text der geschichtliche Bücher des Neuen Testaments", in: ZNW 45 1954, p. 90-108.

R. M. Grant and D. N. Freedman, *The Secret Sayings of Jesus*, London and Glasgow 1960.

J. H. Greenlee, "The Gospel Text of Cyril of Jerusalem", in: *S and D* XVII Copenhagen 1955.

——, *Introduction to New Testament Textual Criticism*, Grand Rapids 1964.

A. Guillaumont, "ΝΗΣΤΕΥΕΙΝ ΤΟΝ ΚΟΣΜΟΝ", in: *Bulletin de l'Institut Français d'archéologie Orientale* 61 1962, p. 15-23.

A. Guillaumont, H.-Ch. Puech, G. Quispel, W. Till and † Yassah ʿAbd Al Masih, *The Gospel according to Thomas, Coptic Text established and translated*, Leiden-London 1959 (also in French and Dutch).

E. Haenchen, "Schriftzitate und Textüberlieferung in der Apostelgeschichte", in: *ZTK* 51 1954, p. 153-167.

——, "Zum Text der Apostelgeschichte", in: *ZTK* 44 1957, p. 22-55.

——, "Die Botschaft des Thomasevangeliums", in: *Theol. Bibl. Töpelmann* 6, Berlin 1961.

——, "Literatur zum Thomasevangelium", in: *TR* 27 1961, p. 147-178 and 306-338.

E. Haenchen and P. Weigandt, "The Original Text of Acts?", in: *NTS* 14 1967/68, p. 469-481.

R. P. C. Hanson, "The Provenance of the Interpolator in the 'Western Text' of Acts and of Acts itself", in: *NTS* 12 1965/66, p. 211-230.

——, "Zu den Evangelienzitaten in den 'Acta Archelai'", in: *Studia Patristica* VII, in: *TU* 92 1966, p. 473-485.

——, "The Ideology of Codex Bezae in Acts", in: *NTS* 4 1967/68, p. 282-286.

W. Henss, "Das Verhältnis zwischen Diatessaron, christlicher Gnosis und 'Westlicher Text'", in: *Beih. ZNW* 33 1967.

A. J. B. Higgins, "The Latin Text of Luke in Marcion and Tertullian", in: *VC* 2 1951, p. 1-42.

——, "The Persian Gospel Harmony as a witness to Tatian's Diatessaron", in: *JTS* n.S. 3 1952, p. 83-87.

——, "The Persian and Arabic Gospel Harmonies", in: *Studia Evangelica*, in: *TU* 73 1959, p. 793-810.

E. F. Hills, "The Inter-Relationship of the Caesarean Manuscripts", in: *JBL* 68 1949, p. 141-159.

H. Hunger, "Zur Datierung des Papyrus Bodmer II (P66) (Mit 1 Tafel)", in: *Anzeiger der phil.-hist. Kl. der Österreichischen Akademie der Wissensch.* 1960, nr. 4, p. 12-23.

C. H. Hunzinger, "Außersynoptischer Traditionsgut im Thomas-Evangelium", in: *TL* 85 1960, c. 843-846.

——, "Unbekannte Gleichnisse Jesu aus dem Thomas-Evangelium", in: *Judentum Christentum Kirche*, Festschrift für J. Jeremias in: *Beih. ZNW* 26, Berlin 1964, p. 209-220.

H. W. Huston, "Mark 6 and 11 in P⁴⁵ and the Caesarean Text", in: *JBL* 74 1955, p. 262-271.

M. Karnetzki, "Textgeschichte als Überlieferungsgeschichte", in: *ZNW* 47 1956, p. 160-180.

[R. Kasser] *Papyrus Bodmer XVII, Actes des Apôtres . . .* Publié par R. Kasser. Bibliotheca Bodmeriana 1961.

——, *L'Évangile selon Thomas*, Neuchâtel 1961.

J. Kerschensteiner, "Beobachtungen zum altsyrischen Actatext", in: *Bibl.* 45 1964, p. 63-74.

R. Kieffer, "Au delà des Recensions? L'Évolution de la Tradition Textuelle dans Jean VI, 52-71", in: *Coniect. Biblica*, New Testament Series 3, Lund 1968.

G. D. Kilpatrick, "The Transmission of the New Testament and its Reliability", in: *945th Ordinary General Meeting of the Victoria Institute*, Croydon, p. 92-101.

——, "An eclectic Study of the Text of Acts", in: *Biblical and Patristic Studies* in Memory of R. P. Casey, ed. by J. N. Birdsall and R. W. Thomson, Freiburg 1963, p. 64-77.

——, "Atticism and the Text of the Greek New Testament", in: *Neutestamentliche Aufsätze*, Festschrift für J. Schmid, Regensburg 1963 p. 125-137.

——, "Style and Text in the Greek New Testament", in: *Studies in the History and Text of the New Testament* in honor of K. W. Clark, in: *S and D* XXIX 1967, p. 153-160.

K. W. Kim, "The Matthean Text of Origin in his Commentary on Matthew", in: *JBL* 68 1949, p. 125-139.

——, "Origen's Text of Matthew in his Against Celsus", in: *JTS* n.S. 4 1953, p. 42-49.

——, "Origen's Text of John in his On Prayer, Commentary on Matthew and Against Celsus", in: *JTS* n.S. 7 1956, p. 74-84.

A. F. J. Klijn, *A Survey of the Researches into the Western Text of the Gospels and Acts*, Utrecht 1949.

——, "An old Witness of the Armenian Text", in: *JTS* 52 1951, p. 168-170.

——, "A Medieval Dutch Text of Acts", in: *NTS* 1 1954/55, p. 51-56.

——, "Papyrus Bodmer II (John I-XIV) and the Text of Egypt", in: *NTS* 3 1956/67, p. 327-334.

——, "A Survey of the Researches into the Western Text of the Gospel and Acts (1949-1959)", in: *NT* 3 1959, p. 1-27 and 161-173.

——, "Het Evangelie van Petrus en de Westerse Tekst", in: *NTT* 15 1960/61, p. 264-269.

——, "Das Thomasevangelium und das altsyrische Christentum", in: *VC* 15 1961, p. 146-159.

——, "In Search of the Original Text of Acts", in: *Studies in Luke-Acts.* Essays presented in honor of P. Schubert, ed. by L. E. Keck and J. L. Martyn, Nashville 1966, p. 103-110.

——, "The Question of the Rich Young Man in a Jewish-Christian Gospel", in: *NT* 8 1966, p. 149-155.

H. Köster, "Synoptische Überlieferung bei den apostolischen Vätern", in: *TU* 65 1957.

——, "ΓΝΩΜΑΙ ΔΙΑΦΟΡΟΙ. The Origin and Nature of Diversification in the History of the Early Christianity", in: *HTR* 58 1965, p. 279-318.

W. Krogmann, "Heliand und Thomasevangelium", in: *ZNW* 51 1960, p. 255-268.

——, "Heliand und Thomasevangelium", in: *VC* 18 1964, p. 65-73.

K. H. KUHN, "Some Observations on the Coptic Gospel according to Thomas", in: *Le Muséon* 73 1960, p. 317-323.

B. LAYTON, "The Sources and Transmission of Didache 1. 3b-2.1", in: *HTR* 61 1968, p. 343-383.

L. LELOIR, "Saint Ephrem Commentaire de l'Évangile Concordant", in: *CSCO* 137, I Louvain 1953; 142, II Louvain 1954.

——, "Le Diatessaron de Tatien", in: *L'Orient Syrien* I 1956, p. 208-231 and 313-334.

—— "L'Évangile d'Éphrem d'après les Oeuvres éditées. Recueil des Textes", in: *CSCO* 180, Subsidia 12, Louvain 1958.

——, L'Original Syriaque du Commentaire de S. Éphrem sur le Diatessaron", in: *Bibl.* 40 1959, p. 959-970.

——, "Témoignage d'Éphrem sur le Diatessaron", in: *CSCO* 227, Subsidia 19, Louvain 1962.

——, "Saint Éphrem, Commentaire de l'Évangile Concordant, Texte Syriaque (Manuscript Chester Beatty 709)". Édité et Traduit par DOM LOUIS LELOIR, in: *Chester Beatty Monographs* No. 8, Dublin 1963.

——, "Divergences entre l'Original Syriaque et la Version Arménienne du Commentaire d'Éphrem sur le Diatessaron", in: *Mél. Eugène Tisserant*, in: *Studi e Testi* 232, Città del Vaticano 1964, p. 303-331.

—— *Éphrem de Nisibe*, "Commentaire de l'Évangile Concordant ou Diatessaron. Traduit du Syriaque et de l'Arménienne", par L. LELOIR, in: *Sourc. Chrét.* 121, Paris 1966.

W. C. LINSS, *The Four Gospel Text of Didymus the Blind*, D. Theol. Boston Univ. 1955.

W. C. LINTON, "Evidences of a second-century revised Edition of St. Mark's Gospel", in: *NTS* 14 1967/68, p. 321-355.

S. LYONNET, "Les Origines de la Version Arménienne et le Diatessaron", in: *BO* 13, Roma 1950.

L. MARIÈS, "Le Diatessaron à l'Origine de la Version Arménienne", in: *RSR* 38 1951, p. 247-256.

——, "Pour l'Étude du Diatessaron", in: *RSR* 44 1956, p. 228-233.

R. P. MARKHAM and E. A. NIDA, *An Introduction to the Bible Societies' Greek New Testament*, publ. by the Sponsoring Societies 1966.

E. MASSAUX, "Le Texte du Sermon sur la Montagne de Matthieu utilisé par Saint Justin", in: *Ephem. Theol. Lovan.* 28 1952.

——, "État actuel de la Critique Textuelle du Nouveau Testament", in: *NRT* 69 1953, p. 703-726.

[V. MARTIN] *Papyrus Bodmer II. Évangile de Jean chap.* 1-14. Publié par VICTOR MARTIN. Bibliotheca Bodmeriana 1956.

——, *Papyrus Bodmer II, Supplément. Évangile de Jean chap.* 14-21. Publié par VICTOR MARTIN. Bibliotheca Bodmeriana. 1958.

——, *Papyrus Bodmer XIV. Évangile de Luc chap.* 3-24. Publié par VICTOR MARTIN et RUDOLPHE KASSER. Bibliotheca Bodmeriana 1961.

——, *Papyrus Bodmer XV. Évangile de Jean chap.* 1-15. Publié par VICTOR MARTIN et RUDOLPHE KASSER. Bibliotheca Bodmeriana 1961.

——, *Papyrus Bodmer II, Supplément Évangile de Jean chap.* 14-21. Publié par VICTOR MARTIN et J. W. B. BARNS. Nouvelle Édition augmentée et corrigée avec reproduction photographique complète du manuscrit (chap. 1-21). Bibliotheca Bodmeriana 1962.

C. M. MARTINI, "Il problema delle recensionalità de Codice B alle luce de papiro Bodmer XIV", in: *Analecta Biblica* 26, Roma 1966.

H. K. McArthur, "The Dependence of the Gospel of Thomas on the Synoptics", in: *ET* 71 1959/60, p. 280-287.
R. McL. Wilson, *Studies in the Gospel of Thomas*, London 1960.
——, "Thomas and the Synoptic Gospels", in: *ET* 72 1960/61, p. 36-39.
M. Mees, *Die Zitate aus dem Neuen Testament bei |Klemens von Alexandrien*, Dissert. Pontif. Instit. Biblic., Roma 1966.
——, "Papyrus Bodmer XIV (P⁷⁵) und die Lukaszitate bei Clemens von Alexandrien", in: *Studi e Recherche di Scienze Religione in onore dei Santi Apostoli Pietro e Paolo nel XIX centenario del loro martirio*, Roma, Facultas Theologica Pontificae Universitatis Lateranensis 1967, p. 97-120.
——, "Die Änderungen und Zusätze im Matthäus-Evangelium des Codex Bezae", in: *Vetera Christianorum* 4 1967, p. 107-129.
P. H. Menoud, "The Western Text and the Theology of Acts", in: *Studiorum Novi Testamenti Societas*, Bulletin II 1951, p. 19-32 .
G. Messina, "Lezioni Apocrifi del Diatessaron Persiano", in: *Bibl.* 30 1949, p. 10-27.
——, "Parallellismi Semitismi Lezioni tendenzioni nell'Armonia Persiano", in: *Bibl.* 30 1949, p. 356-376.
——, "Diatessaron Persiano", in: *BO* 14, Roma 1951.
B. M. Metzger, "The Evidence of the Versions for the Text of the New Testament", in: M. M. Parvis and A. P. Wikgren, *New Testament Manuscript Studies*, Chicago 1948, p. 25-68.
——, "Tatian's Diatessaron and a Persian Harmony of the Gospels", in: *JBL* 69 1950, p. 261-280.
——, "A Survey of recent Research in the ancient Versions of the New Testament", in: *NTS* 2 1955/56, p. 1-116.
——, "Thomas and the Synoptic Gospels", in: *ET* 72 1960/61, p. 36-39.
——, "The Bodmer Papyrus of Luke and John", in: *ET* 73 1961/62, p. 201-203.
——, "The Caesarean Text of the Gospels", in: *Chapters in the History of New Testament Textual Criticism*, in: *NTTS* IV 1963, p. 42-72.
——, "Tatian's Diatessaron and a Persian Harmony of the Gospels", in: *idem*, p. 97-120.
——, *The Text of the New Testament. Its Transmission, Correction and Restauration*, Oxford 1964 (sec. ed. 1968).
——, "Bibliographic Aids to the Study of the Manuscripts of the New Testament", in: *Anglican Theol. Rev.* 48 1966, p. 339-355.
W. Michaelis, "Das Thomas-Evangelium", in: *Calwer Hefte* 34, Stuttgart 1960.
J. Mizzi, "The Latin Text of Matt. V-VII in St. Augustine's 'De Sermone Domini in Monte'", in: *Augustiniana* 4 1954, p. 450-594.
——, "The Latin Text of the Gospel Quotations in St. Augustine's 'De Diversis Quaestionibus LXXXIII Liber Unus'", in: *idem* 12 1962, p. 245-290.
Chr. Mohrmann, "Les Origines de la Latinité Chrétienne à Rome", in: *VC* 3 1949, p. 67-112 and 163-183.
J. Molitor, "Die Georgische Bibelübersetzung", in: *OC* 37 1953, p. 23-29.
——, "Das Adysh-Tetraevangelium", in: *OC* 37 1953, p. 30-35; 38 1954, p. 11-40; 39 1955, p. 1-32; 40 1956, p. 1-15; 41 1957, p. 1-21; 42 1958, p. 1-18; 43 1959, p. 1-16; 44 1960, p. 1-16; 45 1961, p. 1-8; 46 1962, p. 1-18; 47 1963, p. 1-15.
——, "Chanmetifragmente. Ein Beitrag zur Textgeschichte der alt-georgischen Bibelübersetzung", in: *OC* 41 1957, p. 22-34; 43 1959, p. 17-23; 44 1960, p. 17-24; 45 1961, p. 115-126; 46 1962, p. 19-24.

J. Molitor, "Die Bedeutung der altgeorgischen Bibel für die neutestamentliche Textkritik", in: *BZ* 4 1960, p. 39-53.

H. Montefiore, "A Comparison of the Parables of the Gospel acc. to
Thomas and the synoptic Gospels", in: *NTS* 1960/61, p. 220-248.

H. Montefiore and H. E. W. Turner, "Thomas and the Evangelists", in:
Stud. in Bibl. Theol. 35, London 1962.

C. D. F. Moule, "H. W. Moule on Acts IV 25", in: *ET* 65 1953/54, p. 220-221.

H. K. Moulton, "The Present State of New Testament Textual Criticism",
in: *The Bible Translator* 16 1965, p. 193-198.

J. Munck, "Bemerkungen zum Thomasevangelium", in: *Studia Theol.*
14 1960, p. 130-147.

H. S. Murphey, "Eusebius' New Testament Text in the Demonstratio
Evangelica", in: *JBL* 73 1954, p. 162-168.

R. North, "Chenoboskion and Q", in: *CBQ* 24 1962, p. 154-170.

H. H. Oliver, "Present Trends in the Textual Criticism of the New Testament", in: *JBR* 30 1962, p. 308-320.

[I. Ortiz de Urbina] *Biblia Polyglotta Matritensia*, Series VI: *Vetus Evangelium Syrorum et exinde exerptum Diatessaron Tatiani*, editionem
curavit Ignatius Ortiz de Urbina, Matriti 1967.

J. Pairman Brown, "An early Revision of the Gospel of Mark", in: *JBL*
78 1959, p. 215-227.

——, "The Form of 'Q' known to Matthew", in: *NTS* 8 1961/62, p. 27-42.

Th. C. Petersen, "An early Coptic Manuscript of Acts: an unrevised
Version of the ancient so-called Western Text", in: *CBQ* 26 1964,
225-241.

Ch. Perrot, "Un Fragment Christo-Palestinien découvert à Khirbet Mird
(Actes des Apôtres X, 28-29; 32-41)", in: *RB* 79 1963, p. 506-555.

F. P. Pickering, "Christlicher Erzählstoff bei Otfrid und im Heliand", in:
Zeitschr. f. Deutsches Altertum und Deutsche Literatur 85, 1954, p.
262-291.

[D. Plooy] "The Liège Diatessaron . . ." by † D. Plooy and † C. A. Phillips, A. H. A. Bakker, Part VI and VII, in: *Verhandel. der Kon.
Akad. van Wetensch.*, afd. Letterk., nwe Reeks deel XXXI, Amsterdam
1963 and 1965.

C. L. Porter, "An Analysis of the Textual Variation between Pap [75] and
Codex Vaticanus in the Text of John", in: *Studies in the History and
Text of the New Testament* in honor of K. W. Clark by B. L. Daniel
and M. J. Suggs, in: S and D XXIX 1967, p. 71-80.

——, "Papyrus Bodmer XV (P[75]) and the Text of Codex Vaticanus", in:
JBL 81 1962, p. 363-376.

H. Quecke, "Lk 1, 34 in den alten Übersetzungen", in: *Bibl* 44 1963, p.
499-510.

——, "Lk 1, 34 im Diatessaron", in: *Bibl* 45 1964, p. 85-88.

G. Quispel, "The Gospel of Thomas and the New Testament", in: *VC* 11
1957, p. 189-1207.

——, "Some Remarks on the Gospel of Thomas", in: *NTS* 5 1959, p.
276-290.

——, "L'Évangile selon Thomas et le 'Texte Occidentale' du Nouveau
Testament", in: *VC* 14 1960, p. 204-215.

——, "Der Heliand und das Thomasevangelium", in: *VC* 16 1962, p. 121-153.

——, "The Syrian Thomas and the Syrian Macarius", in: *VC* 1962, p. 226-235.

——, "The 'Gospel of Thomas' and the 'Gospel of the Hebrews'", in: *NTS*
12 1965/66, p. 371-382.

G. Quispel, "Makarius, das Thomasevangelium und das Lied von der Perle", in: *Supplem. NT* XV 1967.

——, "The Diatessaron and the Historical Jesus, in: *Studi e Materiali di Storia nelle Religioni* 38 1967, p. 463-472.

——, "The Discussion of Judaic Christianity", in: *VC* 22 1968, p. 81-93.

E. F. Rhodes," An annotated List of Armenian New Testament Manuscripts" in: *Annual Report of Theology*, Monograph Series, vol. I, Ikebukuro, Tokyo, Japan 1959, see addition by A. Wikgren, in: *JBL* 79 1960, p. 52-56.

——, "The Corrections of Papyrus Bodmer II, in: *NTS* 14 1967/68, p. 271-281.

K. T. Schäfer, "Die Zitate in der lateinischen Irenäusübersetzung und ihr Wert für die Textgeschichte des Neuen Testaments", in: *Vom Wort des Lebens*, Festschr. M. Meinertz, in: *Neutestamentl. Abhandl.* 1. Erg. Band 1951, p. 50-59.

——, "Der Ertrag der textkritischen Arbeit am Neuen Testament seit der Jahrhundertwende", in: *BZ* n.F. 4 1960, p. 1-18.

R. Schippers, "De Papyruscodex van Johannes (P⁶⁶)", in: *GTT* 57 1957, p. 33-45.

——, *Het Evangelie van Thomas*, Kampen 1960.

——, "Het Evangelie van Thomas, een onafhankelijke Traditie", in: *GTT* 61 1961, p. 46-54.

W. Schrage, "Das Verhältnis des Thomas-Evangelium zur synoptischen Tradition und zu den koptischen Evangelienübersetzung", in: *Beih. ZNW* 29 1964.

J. Smit Sibinga, "Ignatius and Matthew", in: *NT* 8 1966, p. 263-283.

E. R. Smothers, "Papyrus Bodmer II: an Early Codex of St. John", in: *TS* 18 1957, p. 434-441.

——, "The Readings in Papyrus Bodmer II", in: *HTR* 51 1958, p. 109-122.

G. Strecker, "Das Judenchristentum in den Pseudoklementinen", in: *TU* 70 1958.

M. J. Suggs, "Eusebius' Text of John in the 'Writings against Marcellus'", in: *JBL* 75 1956, p. 137-142.

——, "The Eusebian Text of Matthew", in: *NT* 1 1956, p. 233-245.

R. J. Swanson, *The Gospel Text of Clement of Alexandria*, Ph. D. Diss. Yale University 1956.

[R. V. G. Tasker] *The Greek New Testament*, being the Text translated in the New English Bible 1961, ed. R. V. G. Tasker, Oxford-Cambridge 1964.

V. Taylor, *The Text of the New Testament*, London 1961.

W. C. van Unnik (mit Beiträgen von Joh. Bauer und W. Till), *Evangelien aus dem Nilsand*, Frankfurt am Main 1960.

P. Ortiz Valdivielso, "Un nuevo fragmento siriaco del Commentario de S. Efrén al Diatessaron (P. Palau Rib. 2)", in: *Studia Papyrol.* 5 1966, p. 7-17.

Vetus Latina Institut der Erzabtei Beuron, *Bericht* 1, Beuron/Hohenzollern 1967; *Bericht* 2 1968, and *Bericht* 3 1969.

P. Vielhauer, "Judenchristliche Evangelien", in: Hennecke-Schneemelcher, *Neutestamentliche Apokryphen* Band I, Tübingen 1959, p. 75-108.

H. J. Vogels, "Evangelium Colbertinum", in: *Bonner Bibl. Beitr.* 4: I *Text* and 5: II *Untersuchungen*, Bonn 1953.

——, *Handbuch der Textkritik des Neuen Testaments*, Bonn 1955².

80 BIBLIOGRAPHY

D. VOLTURNO, *Four Gospel Text of Eusebius*, Ph. D. Boston University 1956.
A. VÖÖBUS, "Investigations into the Text of the New Testament used by Rabbula of Edessa", in: *Contrib. of Baltic Univ.* 59, Pinneberg 1947.
——, "Researches on the Circulation of the Peshitta in the Middle of the Fifth Century", in: *idem* 64 1948.
——, "Neue Ergebnisse in der Erforschung der Geschichte der Evangelientexte im Syrischen", in: *idem* 65 1948.
——, "The oldest extant Traces of the Syriac Peshitta", in: *Le Muséon* 63 1950, p. 191-204.
——, "La première Traduction Arménienne des Évangiles", in: *RSR* 37 1950, p. 581-586.
——, "Studies in the History of the Gospel Text in Syria", in: *CSCO* 128, Subsidia 3, Louvain 1951.
——, "A critical Apparatus for the Vetus Syra", in: *JBL* 70 1951, p. 123-128.
——, "Neuentdecktes Textmaterial zur Vetus Syra", in: *TZ* 7 1951, c. 30-38.
——, "Die Spuren eines älteren Äthiopischen Evangelientextes im Lichte der liturgischen Monumente", in: *Papers of the Estonian Theol. Soc. in Exile* 2 1951.
——, "Neue Angaben über die textgeschichtlichen Zustände in Edessa in den Jahren ca 326-340", in: *idem* 3 1951.
——, "Die Evangelienzitate in der Einleitung der Persischen Märtyrerakten", in: *Bibl* 33 1952, p. 222-234.
——, "Zur Geschichte der altgeorgischen Evangelientextes", in: *Papers of the Estonian Theol. Soc. in Exile* 4 1953.
——, "Neue Materialen zur Geschichte der Vetus Syra in den Evangelienhandschriften", in: *Papers of the Estonian Theol. Soc. in Exile* 5 1953.
——, "Das Alter der Peschitta", in: OC 38 1954, p. 1-10.
——, "Early Versions of the New Testament," in: *Papers of the Estonian Theol. Soc. in Exile* 6, 1954.
——, "Completion of the Vetus Syra Project", in: *Biblical Research* 7 1962, p. 49-56.
D. S. WALLACE-HADRILL, "Eusebius and the Gospel Text of Caesarea", in: *HTR* 49 1956, p. 105-114.
P. WEIGANDT, "Zwei Griechisch-Sahidische Acta-Handschriften P[41] und 0236", in: *Materialen zur Neutest. Handschriftenkunde*, herausgeg. v. K. ALAND, in: *Arbeiten z. Neutest. Textforschung* Bd. 3, Berlin 1969, p. 54-95.
J. J. VAN WERINGH, *Heliand and Diatessaron*, Assen 1965, also Dr. JUW FON WERINGHA, "Heliand and Diatessaron", in: *Studia Germanica* V, Assen 1965.
M. WILCOX, *The Semitisms in Acts*, Oxford 1965.
G. S. C. WILLIAMS, *Alterations to the Text of the Synoptic Gospels and Acts*, Oxford 1951.
L. E. WRIGHT, *Alterations of the Words of Jesus as quoted in the Literature of the second century*, Cambridge (Mass.) 1952.
J. D. YODER, "The Language of the Gospel Variants of Codex Bezae", in: *NT* 3 1959, p. 241-248.
——, "Semitisms in Codex Bezae", in: *JBL* 78 1959, p. 317-321.
——, "Concordance to the Distinctive Greek Text of Codex Bezae", in: *NTTS* II, Leiden 1961.
G. ZERVOPOULOS, *The Gospel-Text of Athanasius*, Ph. D. Boston University 1955.
H. ZIMMERMANN, "Papyrus Bodmer II und seine Bedeutung für die Textgeschichte des Johannes-Evangeliums", in: *BZ* n.F. 2 1958, p. 214-243.

NEW TESTAMENT REFERENCES

Matthew		4, 9	25	2, 12	43
3, 16	19	4, 21	10	2, 20	43
4, 5	20	5, 31	25	2, 25	42
5, 11	9	10, 17-18	21	3, 3	41
5, 13	13	10, 20-21	21	3, 19	42
5, 14	10, 13	10, 25	21	3, 30	43
5, 15	10	14, 3	25	3, 33	43
5, 22	20			3, 36	42
5, 45	15	Luke		4, 12	42
5, 39	26	3, 22	19	4, 23	41
5. 40	26	6, 22	9	4, 48	43
5, 41	26	6, 28	14	4, 52	43
5, 42	26	6, 29a	26	6, 10	42
6, 8	24	6, 29b	26	6, 52	43
6, 10	20	6, 30	26	6, 52-71	40
7, 6	13	6, 34	12	6, 60	43
10, 34	14	6, 35	12	6, 64	44
10, 42	25	6, 36	15	7,12	44
11, 25	20	8, 5	12	7, 22	42
11, 27	15	8, 16	10	7, 30	43
12, 48	20	8, 20	20	7, 37	43
12, 49	20	8, 21	21	7, 40	43
12, 50	21	8, 45	25	8, 25	42
13, 4	12	10, 21	20	8, 46	43
13, 25	10	11, 33	10	8, 53	44
13, 45	14	11, 52	14	9, 10	43
15, 13	13	11, 53	14	9, 30	43, 44
16, 2-3	21	12, 13- 21	22	10, 7	45, 46/7
18, 21-22	21	12, 51	14	10, 7-25	45
18, 35	13	14, 16-24	13	10, 8	46/7
19, 12	25	16, 14-15	22	10, 10	46/7
19, 16-17	21	16, 19-31	22	10, 11	45, 46/7, 48
19, 17	15	17, 4	21	10, 12	46/7
19, 20-21	21	18, 18-19	21	10, 15	46/7, 48
19, 24	21	18, 21-22	21	10, 16	46/7
22, 1-4	13	18, 25	21	10, 20	46/7
23, 9	13	24, 39	22	10, 22	46/7
23, 13	14			10, 23	45, 46/7
25, 30	16	John		10, 24	45, 46/7
25, 41	16	1, 13	25	10, 25	45, 46/7, 48
27, 16	22	1,15	40	10, 29	43
		1, 22	43	10, 32	45
Mark		1,27	43	10, 32-11, 10	45
1, 4	19	1, 42	43	10, 33	46/7
1, 10	19	1, 46	42	10, 34	46/7, 48
3, 33	20	2, 2	25	10, 36	42, 46/7
4, 4	12	2, 11	44	10, 38	41, 46/7

Ref	Page	Ref	Page	Ref	Page
10, 39	45	11, 52	45	*Acts*	
10, 40	46/7, 48	11, 54	44, 46/7	1, 23	63
10, 41	46/7	11, 56	46/7	2, 41	61
11, 2	44, 46/7	12, 3	44	4, 25	64
11, 3	46/7	12, 9	42	8, 27-11, 13	56
11, 4	45	12, 2	42	10, 28	58
11, 5	43	12, 16	42, 44	10, 28-29	56
11, 7	46/7	12, 26	43	10, 29	58
11, 19	46/7	12, 31	43	10, 32	58
11, 19-33	46	12, 40	44	10, 32-41	56
11, 22	46, 46/7	13, 5	22	10, 33	58
11, 24	45, 46/7	13, 21	42	10, 34	58
11, 25	45	13, 23	43	10, 35	59
11, 27	46/7	14, 12	43	10, 37	58
11, 28	46/7	14, 14	43	10, 38	58
11, 31	46/7	14, 17	43	10, 39	58
11, 32	46/7	15, 10	43	10, 41	58, 59
11, 33	47	15, 17	44	11, 1-2	63
11, 35	42	15, 25	43	12, 25	64
11, 41	43	18, 12	43	14, 21-15, 5	56
11, 43	45, 46/7	18, 34	43	15, 13-25	56
11, 43-56	45	18, 40	43	15, 26-38	56
11, 44	46/7, 48	19, 4	43	15, 39-17, 25	56
11, 45	47	20, 30	43	21, 14-25	57
11, 50	46/7			24, 27	63
				28, 16	63

REFERENCES TO EARLY CHRISTIAN AUTHORS AND WRITINGS

INDEX OF AUTHORS